# THE
# CALNE BRANCH

BY
COLIN G. MAGGS

WILD SWAN PUBLICATIONS LTD.

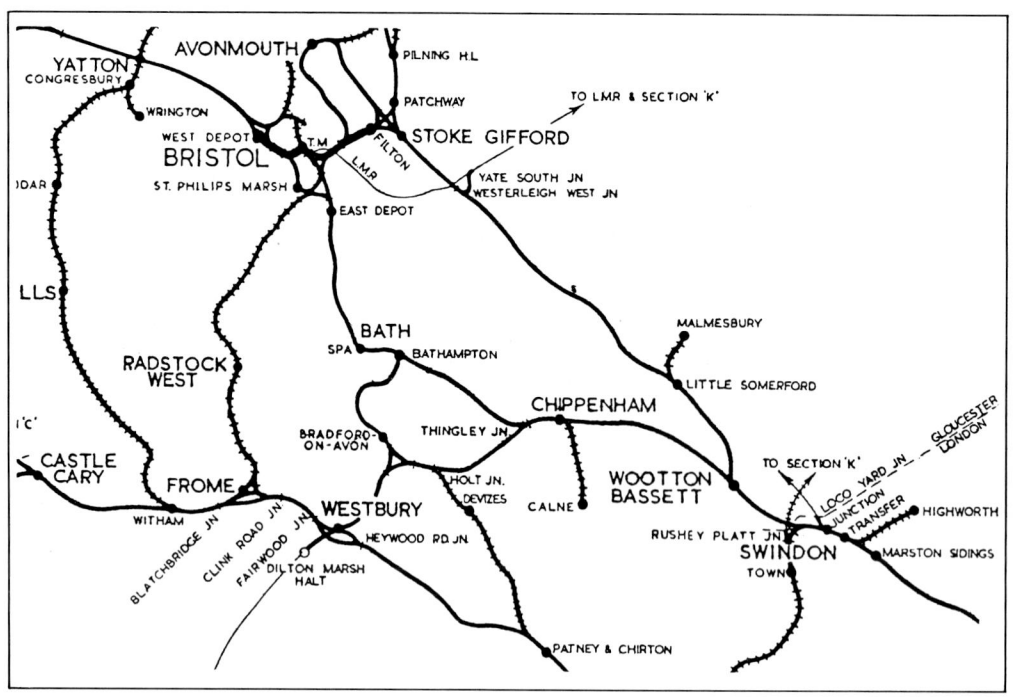

## ACKNOWLEDGEMENTS

Grateful acknowledgement for assistance is due to: Rev. B. Arman; J. Armstrong; O.E. Britton; Calne Town Council; F. & J. Cannon; Dr J. Chandler, Wiltshire Libraries & Museum Local Studies Officer; J. Clapp; A. Cockram; J. Croker; E. Culley; J. Cummings; M.E.J. Deane; Dr A.J.G. Dickens; E. Edwards; H. Evans; M. Fell; C. Gale; S. Hawkins; E.J.M. Hayward; F. Howarth; D.J. Hyde; M.R. Johnson, Westinghouse Brake & Signal Co. Ltd; R. Jones; R. Kelham; K. Leech; H. Longshaw; D. Lovelock; I. Pett; W. Read; F.B. Simpkins, Yelde Hall Museum, Chippenham; C. Skull; A. Slade; F. Stapleford; D.R. Steggles; M.J. Tozer; P.Q. Treloar; P. Vines; J. Whiles; B. White; Wiltshire Record Office.

R. Ball, G.B. Hunt and D. Warboys have special thanks for checking the manuscript.

© Wild Swan Publications Ltd. and Colin G. Maggs 1990
ISBN 0 906867 89 4

Designed by Paul Karau
Printed by Amadeus Press Ltd., Huddersfield

Published by
WILD SWAN PUBLICATIONS LTD.
1-3 Hagbourne Road, Didcot, Oxon. OX11 8DP

## Bibliography

Ashworth C. *Action Station Vol. 5* (Patrick Stephens)
*Bradshaw's Railway Manual, Shareholders' Guide & Directory 1869* (David & Charles)
Calne Railway Minute Books
Clark R.H. *An Historical Survey of Selected Great Western Stations Vol. 3* (Oxford Publishing Co.)
Clinker C.R. *Closed Stations & Goods Depots* (Avon Anglia)
Cooke R.A. *Track Layout Diagrams of the GWR and BR WR, Section 21.* (Author)
Cummings J. *Railway Motor Buses & Bus Services 1902-33* (Oxford Publishing Co)
Dalby L.J. *The Wilts & Berks Canal* (Oakwood Press)
Daniell J.J. *The History of Chippenham* (Houlston)
Leigh C. *GWR Country Stations, No. 2* (Ian Allan)
Leleux S.A. *Brotherhoods, Engineers* (David & Charles)
*Locomotives of the Great Western Railway* (Railway Correspondence & Travel Society)
Lyons E. & Mountford E. *An Historical Survey of Great Western Engine Sheds 1837-1947* (Oxford Publishing Co.)
Lyons E. *An Historical Survey of Great Western Engine Sheds 1947* (Oxford Publishing Co.)
Marsh A.E.W. *A History of the Borough & Town of Calne* (R.S. Heath)
Marshall J. *A Biographical Dictionary of Railway Engineers* (David & Charles)
Platts A. *History of Chippenham* (Author)
Tanner G. *The Calne Branch* (Oxford Publishing Co.)
Tyler R.J. *Some Aspects of the Roads of the Calne Trust 1773-1871* (Author)
*Victoria County History of Wiltshire, Vol 4* (Oxford University Press)
Newspapers: *Bath Chronicle*; *Devizes & Wiltshire Gazette*; *North Wilts Herald*; *Swindon Advertiser*
Magazines: *Engineering*; *Great Western Magazine*; *Railway Magazine*; *Railway Observer*; *Trains Illustrated*.

# INTRODUCTION

Dating from Saxon times, Calne is a small and lively market town, some of the famous names associated with the borough including Lord Macaulay, historian, essayist and politician, and Joseph Priestley, librarian at Bowood House, who discovered oxygen while residing there. Samuel Taylor Coleridge, poet, critic and drug addict, also lived in the town from 1815–1817. The industrial career of Calne fell into two phases: the ancient cloth weaving industry and the bacon curing business of Messrs Harris. The hand weaving of cloth ceased about 1835 owing to competition from the increasing use of steam power in the North of England, but the bacon industry developed and continued to thrive through the nineteenth century and the first half of the twentieth century, to such an extent that Calne and bacon were almost as synonymous as Sheffield and steel.

Calne first appeared in history circa 955 when mentioned in the will of King Edred who died that year. The Wiltshire Downs was great sheep-rearing country and, until the fourteenth century, cloth was made only for local use, but then, for five centuries, fabric became an important industry.

The name of Harris first became associated with bacon curing circa 1808 when John and Henry Harris set up shop, but it was under John's sons, Thomas, George and Henry, that Calne really became known as a bacon town. Before the Great Western Railway opened, large numbers of Irish pigs were conveyed by sea to Bristol and then driven to London via Calne. This pig droving was thoroughly organised, with regular stops for rest, Calne being within the stage from Black Dog Hill, 1½ miles west of the town, to Overton, 8 miles east. At the end of each stage, large sheds were provided for pig accommodation. Most of the early bacon cured at Calne came from these pigs.

When the Irish potato famine of 1845 and 1846 caused this supply of pigs to run nearly dry, it looked as if the Calne bacon business faced ruination, so George sailed for America, intending to breed, kill and cure pigs there and send them to England. However, after some initial success, his business failed and he returned to Calne, but his trip had not been fruitless, as in the United States George had observed the use of ice as a preserving agent. He realised the great potential of using it in bacon curing, for cooling would permit the process to be carried on throughout the summer months, instead of being limited to the winter and having to keep bacon hard salted for summer use. George Harris collected ice locally in bad winters, and imported from Norway when it was unobtainable in England.

Charles disapproved of this innovation, but George and Thomas patented their special ice house which gave them a lead over all other bacon curers, so that in addition to profits accruing from their own curing, they received royalties from other English and Irish manufacturers who adopted their ice house. Their businesses flourished and by 1887 bacon was being exported by them to most European countries, the USA, Australia, New Zealand, India, China, and the Cape of Good Hope. The two Harris companies merged in 1888. Just before Christmas 1878 1½ miles of sausages had been made, while the following year about 2,000 pigs were killed weekly by the two Harris factories. By 1900 some 120,000 pigs were slaughtered annually. Before 1914, in addition to bacon, Messrs Harris produced sausages, sausage meat, cooked luncheon sausage, meat pies, polonies, Bath chaps, saveloys, galatine of ham and tongue in glass, while the post World War I period saw an even greater variety made of sausages, pies, cooked meats, meat and fish paste and specialities in glass and tins. During the Second World War the firm supplied the armed forces with large quantities of tinned and fresh food.

A by-products factory was built in 1930 to produce fertiliser, feeding stuffs, soap stock, material for medicinal products, curled hair for upholstery and bristles for brushes. The number of personnel employed grew from 651 in 1917 to 1,113 in 1927 and 2,116 in 1957.

**Population of Calne**

| 1861 | 1871 | 1881 | 1891 | 1901 | 1911 | 1921 | 1931 | 1951 | 1961 |
|---|---|---|---|---|---|---|---|---|---|
| 2,494 | 2,468 | 2,474 | 3,495* | 3,457 | 3,538 | 3,640 | 4,359 | 5,553 | 6,574 |

* Area altered to include the Calne Urban Sanitary District

Chippenham, first mentioned by name in 853, and six miles west of Calne along the Bath Road, was the seat of King Alfred until he was forced by the Danish invaders to retreat to Athelney in Somerset, but he returned victorious after making the Peace of Wedmore. Chippenham became important because of the bridge over the Avon and since Saxon days, it has had a market where fine crops of wheat and barley grown on the Wiltshire Downs were sold. From the reign of Elizabeth I till the end of the eighteenth century, cloth was important and in 1790 there were still about sixty busy and prosperous cloth factories at Chippenham. These were not factories in the modern sense, but shops where fabric was finished, the earlier processes being carried out by families in their own cottages. Colliers from Somerset took sacks of coal by packhorse and mule to Chippenham and returned loaded with corn and cloth. Power looms established in large factories of Lancashire and Yorkshire dealt an almost fatal blow, with riots at Chippenham in 1801 and 1802 nearly putting an end to the industry. 1838 saw the town's weavers in great distress – only 31 at work out of 86, even those who were fortunate enough to be employed being very poorly paid. The industry completely ceased in 1915 when the last mill burnt out.

When a stage coach service Bristol–Bath–London started circa 1650, the journey occupied three days, but by 1722, the fastest coach had reduced this time to two days, and by the end of the seventeenth century a small spa had been established at Chippenham.

In 1842 Rowland Brotherhood, a railway building contractor, set up a smith's shop to repair maintenance tools, and from this grew his Chippenham Railway Works situated to the north of the passenger station. On completion of the Great Western line and until 1861, Brotherhood held contracts for maintaining earthworks and permanent way for 350 miles of line. The works expanded from just manufacturing tools and permanent way fittings, to constructing signalling equipment, by the Westinghouse King's Cross works. Today the firm owns a 46 acre site, 20 acres of which are occupied by buildings. The 600 employees at Chippenham in 1919, grew to 1,700 in 1929 and 2,700 in 1938.

Another important industry at Chippenham was the Anglo-Swiss Condensed Milk Company, later Nestlés Milk Products Ltd, established in 1873, producing sweetened condensed milk in premises which were originally a cloth factory built by T. Goldney, clothier, in 1802. Right from the beginning condensed milk was manufactured at Chippenham on a large scale. The initial workforce of 53 men and 12 women grew to 131 by 1886, 163 in 1906 and 213 in 1937.

Hathaway Brothers had a milk churn factory manufacturing for export as well as for home use. Packing cases for dispatch were made by Messrs Downing, Radman & Beint who worked in adjacent premises. Messrs Hathaway's factory closed about 1937.

Of the 5,000 workers at Chippenham in 1939, 2,277 were employed in engineering, the majority of these by the Westinghouse Brake & Signal Co; about 580 worked in the food industry – Nestlés milk products, Oxo Ltd, and the Wiltshire Bacon Co, while 112 were in transport and communication.

| **Population** | 1861 | 1871 | 1881 | 1891 | 1901 | 1911 | 1921 | 1931 | 1951 | 1961 |
|---|---|---|---|---|---|---|---|---|---|---|
| Chippenham Municipal Borough | 1,603 | 1,387 | 1,352 | 4,618 | 5,074 | 5,332 | 7,710 | 9,461 | 14,941 | 17,543 |
| Chippenham Urban Sanitary District | — | — | 4,495 | | | | | | | |

railway wagons and bridges, some 400 men being employed. He opened a locomotive works at Chippenham about 1858, his first engine probably being the broad gauge 0-6-0 tank engine *Moloch*. Between 1862 and 1867 about fifteen standard gauge saddle tank engines were built, probably to the design of his son Peter. Although he could have weathered the financial storm in 1869, the North Wilts Bank forced the business to be sold, the works closing on 17th March 1869, causing the fall in population between the 1861 and 1871 censuses. In January 1871 Joseph Armstrong, the Great Western locomotive superintendent, rented the works for use as carriage sheds and in 1894 the building was acquired by Evans O'Donnell. Eventually taken over by the Wiltshire Bacon Curing Company, they were closed and burnt down in 1987.

A signal works started by Evans O'Donnell & Co Ltd in 1894 was acquired nine years later by Saxby & Farmer, who brought in their own workers and plant from Kilburn, London. In 1920 the company merged with the Westinghouse Brake Co Ltd of King's Cross, N. McKenzie & Holland of Worcester, and McKenzie, Holland & Westinghouse Power Signal Co Ltd, these four firms combining to form the Westinghouse Brake & Saxby Signal Co Ltd. At the same time, McKenzie & Holland's plant moved to Chippenham, followed in 1932

When canals were proposed in order to encourage and develop trade to an extent impossible using the existing poor roads, August 1789 saw Robert Whitworth reporting favourably on an undertaking planned to link the River Kennet, via Hungerford, Marlborough, Calne and Chippenham, with the Avon at Bath. Although this particular project failed through lack of financial support, in the event the Kennet & Avon Canal took a more southerly route via Pewsey and Devizes. Chippenham and Calne were each served by a short branch from the Wilts & Berks Canal, the main line of which passed approximately midway between the two towns. One of the objects of the undertaking was to carry Somerset coal. The Calne branch was opened by the end of 1802 and that to Chippenham about the same time, the whole waterway being completed through to the Thames on 10th September 1810. It is recorded that in 1837 4,709 tons of coal were carried on the Chippenham branch and 3,695 on that to Calne. Bricks were another important commodity transported by the canal.

The Great Western Railway reached Chippenham on 31st May 1841 and opened through to Bath and Bristol a month later on 30th June. In 1845 a rival line, the London, Bristol & South Wales Direct Railway, was proposed, which would have passed through Calne, but this plan proved abortive.

# CHAPTER ONE
# PROPOSALS AND CONSTRUCTION

THE principal inhabitants of Calne realised that the value of their trade would improve if a railway was opened to the town, and there was certainly sufficient traffic to warrant a line being built, for sixteen mills were within three miles of Calne, quite apart from the largest bacon business in England. The latter particularly needed a rapid modern transport system to assemble its raw materials – pigs, salt, ice and coal – and to distribute the bacon and sausages before their quality deteriorated.

A public meeting was called at the Town Hall on 8th November 1859, nearly all the leading residents being present. The scheme's sole opponent was James C. Hale, a local wharfinger and coal merchant, who for his own business reasons, obviously did not wish to see any transport rivalling that of the canal. This meeting passed the resolution 'That it is highly desirable and will prove very advantageous to Calne and the neighbourhood to have a line of railway from the town to join the Great Western Railway at or near Chippenham station'. It was revealed that transport between Calne and Chippenham cost Harris's bacon factory about £800 a year and this sum would help swell the railway's receipts. The meeting resulted in a promised subscription of about £15,000.

James Baird Burke was appointed engineer and estimated the cost of the line to be £26,663. James Samuel accepted the post of joint engineer on 19th November at a fee of £1,925. Samuel, born in Glasgow and educated at its University, had been resident engineer of the Eastern Counties Railway in 1846 and patented a rail fish joint. Latterly he became concerned in various overseas railways and an advocate of light rolling stock.

The first meeting of the promoters recorded in the Calne Railway Minute Book (which was unusual in being smaller than the foolscap size normally used, its pages measuring only 9in by 7½in) was held on 3rd November 1859 at the offices of Clarkson & Rogers, Calne. Thomas Large Henly took the chair. Present were William John Dowding, Charles, George, Henry and Thomas Harris, the Harris's subscribing more than half the capital. Clarkson & Rogers were appointed the company's solicitors and Henry Weaver given the post of surveyor at a fee of £125.

The GWR secretary sent a letter dated 2nd November:

'Having now examined the whole subject with much care, I am desired to inform you that the Directors entertain doubts whether the Revenue of that proposed Branch can for some years be sufficient for the necessary working Charges and also remunerative for the Outlay and Capital. This consideration becomes very important in the proposal of Terms and Conditions for working the line, even although this Company cannot, as the Directors informed your Deputation, become contributors of Capital.'

During the first two years, the GWR promised to charge the cost price only and work the line without profit, in subsequent years using the following scale:

*Gross Revenue*   *Percentage of gross revenue taken for working expenses*

Less than £10 per week  60%
£10 to £15   ,,   ,,   57%
Exceeding £15   ,,   ,,   52½%

(This table was slightly modified at a Heads of Agreement meeting between the two companies on 27th May 1862, the document signed two days later.)

Unfortunately, the principal landowner, the Marquess of Lansdowne, not at all confident of the line's success, wrote to the Calne Railway promoters intimating this and indicating that he did not wish to take a leading part in the scheme, but adding that if he received evidence that a large number of people supported the project, he would, 'not for his own interest, but out of respect for them, subscribe'.

Neither of the local banks, the North Wilts Banking Co., Melksham, nor the Wilts & Dorset Banking Co., Salisbury, would take shares, but, as some of the directors of the former took thirty shares between them, this company was appointed the railway's bankers.

At first it was thought that there would be no intermediate station, but then the desirability of one at Stanley was discussed and the matter left open for further consideration, though, in the event, the proposal was rejected.

On 14th December, James Samuel, joint engineer, sent a letter to the directors saying that his estimate for the line (£32,000) was £7,000 in excess of that submitted by his co-engineer James Burke (£26,663) and expressed a wish to withdraw from the undertaking, presumably not wanting to be associated with an underfunded line. This led the directors to offer unusual terms to Burke on 20th December. It was proposed that he would be appointed sole engineer if he agreed to a fee of £1,950 and assented to receiving only a half fee (i.e. £1,000) if the line, including the station at Calne, was not ready for traffic for £27,000. Burke accepted this offer, saying that he would find a contractor to build the line for this sum, including £2,000 for a goods and passenger station at Calne, and that the contractor would take £5,000 in shares as part payment. On 29th December these terms were modified, Burke agreeing to a payment of £1,650 reduced to £1,000 if the line cost in excess of £27,000.

The contractor, Richard Hattersley of Nursling, Southampton, and contractor for the Andover & Redbridge Railway, attended the directors' meeting in Clarkson & Roger's office on 30th January 1860 and agreed to construct the line for £27,000, taking £5,000 of this payment in shares. Then, on understanding that this price included the goods and passenger stations, he withdrew his offer. The meeting then adjourned to the Lansdowne Arms Hotel where he was staying and, following discussions, Hattersley agreed to build the line for £26,000 exclusive of stations, and take £7,000 in shares as part payment. This was on the Calne Railway undertaking that if a sufficient quantity of ballast could not be obtained from land purchased by the company, Hattersley would be empowered to buy it elsewhere and be allowed £100 over and above the £26,000. The contract stated that Hattersley was to lay single broad gauge track, construct not more than four bridges, one timber viaduct 53 yards in length over the Avon, and provide twenty occupation crossings. Hattersley ended his survey with the engineer, Burke, on 30th January, signing the contract on 1st February. A local builder undertook to erect the station buildings at Calne.

By 18th April the value of shares subscribed amounted to nearly £19,000. The Marquess of Lansdowne in a letter of 7th May wrote of Hattersley:

'... that although there is nothing to be stated against his personal character, he is not a person of any substance, or possessed at present of means equal to meet so large an advance as he proposed to make. Under these circumstances I might consider myself absolved from the promise which I continually make.'

Lansdowne said he would invest £1,000 but requested that no capital be made from his name. Furthermore, he expected a clause inserted in the company's bill providing for a station at the foot of Chilvester Hill (near the later Black Dog Halt), as he anticipated inconvenience if the railway caused the canal to fall into disuse. The directors replied saying that his contribution was so small as to preclude the possibility of complying with his wish to have a station erected.

The bill was put to Parliament, the preamble proved, and it passed to the Commons Committee on 28th February. The Act, 23–4, Vic c.11, received Royal Assent on 15th May 1860, authorising a capital of £35,000 and loans of £11,600. The Act stipulated that a £50 per day penalty would be incurred if the Wilts & Berks Canal was obstructed. An unusual clause required the length of the viaduct over the Avon to be a minimum of 60 yards – slightly longer than that laid down in Hattersley's contract. Completion of the line was required within four years. The cost of obtaining the Act was £1,412 9s. 7d. less than contemplated but it would have been even £230 cheaper had the company been spared costs of contending petitions against the bill. By 28th May only £5,000 worth of shares remained to be taken.

At the first meeting of the company, as opposed to the Provisional Committee, Henly was appointed chairman, and the first shareholders' meeting held on 13th August. In their report, the directors said that they regretted 'that the undertaking has not received greater support from the landed proprietors of the neighbourhood, the Marquess of Lansdowne and Mr Esmeade being the only landowners who have as yet taken shares'. Although £4,500 still awaited subscription, the directors felt able to go ahead in confidence and purchase the land, Hattersley anticipating that the works would be completed twelve months after cutting the first turf. To be a director, a person needed to hold thirty £10 shares. Those appointed to the Board were George Bailey, William John Dowding, Thomas Harris, Robert Henly and Thomas L. Henly. It was agreed that Charles, George and Henry Harris would still be invited to directors' meetings, although not officially on the board, limited to five seats by the Act. John Nelson Ladd was appointed secretary at an annual salary of £20. A committee of shareholders was elected to work with the directors in selling the remaining shares and on 31st August the directors resolved that no works would be commenced until all the shares had been taken up. This upset Hattersley's arrangements as he was geared up ready to start work, so on 4th September he wrote pointing out that the cost of labour and materials was rising and that it was important to him that the line was commenced immediately. He explained that when he took the contract, Burke, the engineer, had promised that work would begin that July. With this date in mind he had made preparations and had purchased permanent way and sleepers. However, no start was made and at the beginning of October Hattersley offered to take an additional £2,000 in shares, making a total of £9,000, if the directors increased the contract price to £27,000. After carefully considering this proposal, they agreed, subject to him taking £10,000 in shares. Hattersley consented to this on 10th October. The directors artfully contrived to save the extra £1,000 expenditure by proposing a deviation to meet this amount. Had the plan been accepted by Parliament, the junction with the GWR would have been half a mile nearer Swindon, but the Reverend Ashe of Langley Burrell strongly opposed the deviation, forcing the scheme to be abandoned. By mid January 1861, £500–£600 worth of shares were still awaiting sale, but most of these were taken following an appeal at the Annual General Meeting on 20th March.

At this meeting it was stated that Hattersley had yet to start on the contract as he had failed to furnish the names of his sureties to the amount of £10 per cent of his contract – presumably Lansdowne's letter caused this requirement to be inserted. The contract was eventually sealed on 12th June 1861 and it is likely that there were no sureties, the directors finding they had no right to insist on them.

Only about 150 persons were present when the first sod was turned in J. Angell's field, Studley, at 3 p.m. on 25th June 1861, the ceremony being carried out by a principal shareholder, the Rt. Hon. Robert Lowe MP, the Earl of Shelburne declining. One unusual feature of the occasion was that each director dug a sod, while another uncommon occurrence was that the wheelbarrow and spade, instead of being presented to the person who turned the first turf, was donated to Angell, owner of the field, 'as a token', said Charles Harris, 'of their high esteem and respect for the gentleman, and their appreciation of the readiness with which he had given the company possession of his land to commence their undertaking – a readiness which contrasted strikingly, he was sorry to say, with the conduct of other persons, whose eye to the filling of their own pockets had somewhat thwarted the original intention of the Directors as regarded the point at which their operations should commence'. Following the ceremony, the directors and officials dined at the White Hart Hotel, Calne.

On 17th January 1862 the engineer reported that about 50 tons of permanent rails had been placed on the line, while on 26th March he said that at Chippenham, a temporary junction had been made with the GWR to deliver permanent rails and materials for the timber viaduct over the Avon. The viaduct itself was in a forward state and expected to be finished in time for the contractor to take advantage of the summer weather and push the embankment across the valley without risk of it slipping. The Wilts & Berks Canal engineers had approved the bridge across their canal between Studley and Stanley and construction was to commence immediately. Between the canal and the foot of Black Dog Hill, works were being proceeded with in several places. Abutments for the bridge across the turnpike road (the present A4) had been built and, as soon as the iron girders were fixed, Burke anticipated that the embankment would be rapidly completed.

The railway company was fortunate in finding an excellent bed of stone on land owned by Benjamin Bailey, a Calne corn dealer and owner of Calne town corn mill and another at

Berhills, Calne. It provided sufficient to build all the bridges except one; enough to make all roads and to ballast the line in its entirety.

Excavating near Stanley Abbey, the contractor turned up the remains of several skeletons and 'many curious old coins'.

27th May saw the directors travelling to Paddington to work out a Heads of Agreement. Signed the following day, it was to last for ten years. For the first two years the Great Western was to be paid a cash price for working and maintenance, locomotive charges being restricted to an annual maximum of £1,000. To keep within this limit, only one engine with driver and fireman, working for about twelve hours daily, was to be provided, carriage and wagon hire being kept within £200 per annum during the initial two years. Charges after this period were to be:

| Total Weekly receipts per Mile | Calne Railways's Proportion of Receipts |
|---|---|
| Less than £10 | 40% |
| More than £10 | 42½% |
| More than £12 10 0 | 45% |
| More than £20 | 47½% |

In this agreement, signed 29th May, the GWR undertook to provide station accommodation at Chippenham and to run sufficient trains on the branch to develop traffic. Sir Daniel Gooch said the agreement was regarded as exceptionally favourable to the Calne Company and did not stipulate any payment for the use of Chippenham station.

On 13th June the Calne directors heard that about half of the required land had been purchased and the last call on shares had been paid 'with a trifling exception', and were told that the authorised loan of £11,600 would need taking up to add to the amount raised by shares. To forward this, an extraordinary meeting for shareholders was called on 1st August to give consent to the Great Western Working Agreement and to authorise the directors to raise the mortgage necessary to complete the line. On 13th September the engineer reported that if the weather continued favourable and present progress was maintained, he anticipated that all excavation and masonry would be completed within about three months.

Michael Lane, Chief Engineer to the GWR, inspected the Calne Railway on 29th September accompanied by Burke. Lane reported:

'On the whole the works are fairly constructed. The Embankments and Cuttings so far as expected stand well; the latter in one or two cases to a small extent should have the Slopes flattened which Mr Burke at once ordered the contractor to carry into effect. The Slopes for the Embankments require some additional amount of Soiling; there is plenty of Soil on the Line to do this without incurring any additional expense ... Masonry of Bridges and Culverts appeared very good and substantial work ... One bridge with timber decking and another with Cast Iron Trough Girders want some trifling additions to the Deck planking. The Wrought and Cast Iron girders seem well proportioned and of proper strength.

'The timber viaduct over the River Avon at or near Chippenham – I have no fault to find with the workmanship or quality of the materials. The Girders and Planking both require strengthening. This I propose should be done by diagonal strutting to Girders and the planking to be 8in thick instead of 4 as at present.

'Fencing – This is formed of wood posts and Galvanised Iron Wire Strand which I believe is of good quality. The posts, though they are good, are much smaller in scantling or Section than those now in use on the Great Western Railway, in addition to which they have not been creosoted, or prepared in any way, which will diminish their value of life considerably.'

At the shareholders' meeting on 30th September it was reported that Hattersley had made considerable progress with works. The Calne Railway was very fortunate in this respect, as many lines suffered delays due to poor weather, or financial problems. Cash received on calls amounted to £14,040 and the amount drawn on debenture bonds was £11,600, making a total of £25,640. Expenses had been £19,334 17s. 0d.

On 10th October Burke itemised the expenditure required in addition to the £27,000 paid to Hattersley:

|  | £ |
|---|---|
| Extra bridge at Stanley | 800 |
| Extra bridge for Mr Keevil | 1,000 |
| Extra bridge for Lord Crewe | 250 |
| Increase on masonry for cattle creeps etc | 500 |
|  | 2,550 |

|  | £ |  |
|---|---|---|
| Engine house for one engine | 300 |  |
| Goods shed | 500 |  |
| Booking office, platform, etc | 400 |  |
| Water arrangements, tank etc | 400 |  |
|  | 1,600 |  |
|  |  | 1,600 |
| Sidings at station |  | 750 |
|  |  | 4,900 |
| Metalling yards, approaches |  | 350 |
|  |  | 5,250 |

Because of the very wet weather, in January 1863 Hattersley felt unable to name a completion date. On 6th February the directors advanced £600 to him for an engine to help with ballasting, with the proviso that he had it in use within a month. Tenders for erecting station buildings at Calne were advertised in February, submission having to be made by 6th March. Those received were:

|  | £ |
|---|---|
| Henry W. Penning, Pewsey | 1,000 |
| James Davis & Son, Frome | 700 |
| I. Taylor, Bradford on Avon | 633 5s. 0d |
| William Webb, Calne | 567 |

Webb's tender was accepted. Broken down it was:

|  | £ |
|---|---|
| Booking office | 189 |
| Goods shed | 156 |
| Engine house | 147 |
| Water tank | 75 |
|  | 567 |

In his March report Burke stated that progress over the last two months had been very good, and both earthworks and masonry were very considerably advanced. Hattersley's engine had been used for ballasting, and the contractor had undertaken to have the line ready for traffic by 18th June, by which date Webb would have the station buildings ready – he must have thought that Webb would be a quick worker. All land needed for the line had been bought and a siding was to be laid at Black Dog.

Although everything seemed to be going well, at the directors' meeting on 6th June it was revealed that no less than £10,000–£11,000 was required for completing the line, though unfortunately the minute book gives no clue as to how and why this discrepancy arose. Hattersley proposed that if the directors would grant him £1,000 as compensation for the extra excavations and would raise £2,000 on their personal security, he would provide £8,000 in Lloyds bonds for 12 months at the rate of ten per cent discount. The directors responded by saying that they did not feel like giving their personal security on behalf of the company. Thomas Stephenson, Hattersley's solicitor, staying in the town, wrote:

Lansdowne Arms<br>Calne<br>6 June 1863

Gentlemen,

Referring to the very unsatisfactory interview with you this morning in regard to the payment of money due in Mr Burke's certificate of work done during the past month in which you stated you had no funds at your disposal, Mr Hattersley desires me to request you to hand over to me on or before Wednesday next the 10th instant at noon, a cheque for the amount above referring to, and at the same time give me an assurance that the money will be forthcoming to meet the current expenses of the present month, and in the event of your not doing so, he will consider you to have broken your contract, and he shall then be compelled, although reluctantly, to order the suspension of the works and will hold you responsible for all loss and damage occurring thereby.

I am Gentlemen,<br>Your obedient servant,<br>Thomas Stephenson

This letter resulted in Hattersley being paid in Lloyds Bonds on 10th June, a supplementary contract with him being signed on 30th June. The Calne Railway had already paid Hattersley £4,181 for extra works due to serious and continual slips of earth at one part of the works which had not been foreseen by either party when construction was planned, but which the contractor at great cost to himself had made good. He alleged that if the company was not legally, it was morally bound to make him further payment on that account. This supplementary contract said that the Calne Railway would pay Hattersley £5,161, £1,111 to be paid in respect of slips of earth made good and the remainder for signalling at Calne and excavation, metalling, fencing, gates, asphalt to the platforms at Calne station, yard and approaches.

Michael Lane, Chief Engineer to the GWR, wrote to the Calne Railway directors on 17th June saying that he had complained to Burke regarding the condition of sleepers, fencing, ballast and finishing of cuttings. Burke had promised these faults would be brought before the Board, but when Lane met Mr Harris, a Calne Railway director, accidentally on a Metropolitan train, he discovered this had not been done. Lane said that the sleepers were all of 'the most common and cheapest kind called white wood'. Despite the supplier pointing out to Hattersley that they were not fit for the purpose, he was determined to have them. Lane had written to Burke on 5th June saying that the sleepers were too small in scantling 9in by 4in, some 9in by 5in, averaging 9in by 4½in. Many were not rectangular but half round and Lane could not consent to pass them:

'All laid very badly and very irregularly as to distance and out of square, that is, not at right angles with rails, many nine or ten inches out. The ballasting is not by any means up to the mark, the bottom ballast is formed of stone generally very good as to quality, but put on a great deal too large, in short, unbroken having been put on the line as it was got out of the cutting. The top ballast to which I objected when I last accompanied you to Chippenham to examine the viaduct, is entirely worthless, the use of which I cannot sanction.'

Cutting drainage was quite inadequate, there being no provision of side ditches for removing rainfall. The fence posts were too small and not creosoted, and he criticised the wire for not being of the best quality, this seemingly being overlooked in his letter of 25th September 1862. Lane found that the viaduct over the Avon had not yet been strengthened. The contents of Lane's letter suggest that either Burke was not a very thorough engineer, or that he tried to carry out the work too cheaply. Following so shortly after the communication from Hattersley, this letter must have been a bombshell to the directors.

They replied to Lane on 4th July, apologising for the differences between Burke and him. They proposed that the cost and maintenance of works should be borne by the Calne Railway for two years and, if at the expiration of that period objections were made by the GWR or himself, those questions should be referred to arbitration. Presumably the thinking behind the suggestion was that the directors hoped it would defer matters until a time when they hoped the fortunes of the company would be able to pay for improvements.

The Calne Railway directors inquired specialised details from H. Stallard, superintendent of the goods station at Chippenham, and were informed that the delivery of goods and parcels at Chippenham by the GWR brought receipts of £86 over six months, against expenses for one man and two horses of £104. During the same period the GWR had delivered at Calne 158 tons at five shillings a ton, making £39 10s. 0d. against the expenditure of £52 for a horse and man. Having considered these figures, the directors decided not to undertake delivery themselves, but to appoint William Bleadon of the White Hart, Calne, as delivery agent.

Captain Tyler, Royal Engineers, inspected the line on 15th September on behalf of the Board of Trade, making the following report:

The Secretary                                        Whitehall
  Board of Trade                     17 September 1863
    Whitehall
Sir,

I have the honor [*sic*] to report for the information of the Lords of the Committee of Privy Council for Trade, that in compliance with the instructions contained in your letter of the 21st ultimo I have inspected the Calne Railway. I was required by the Engineer of the line to postpone my visit to a later date after the Company had given formal notice for opening it; and this, as well as great pressure of work in other directions, has prevented me from previously going over the line.

It is a branch 5¼ miles long connecting the Town of Calne with the Chippenham Station of the Great Western Railway. The line is single and no land has been purchased nor other arrangements made with a view to doubling it at a future period.

The permanent way has been laid on the broad gauge of 7ft 0¼in. The rails are of the ⊥ section and weigh 66lbs to the lineal yard. They are fished at the joints with wrought iron plates and bolts and nuts; and are secured to transom sleepers by means of cast iron chairs at the joint, and cast iron clips at the intermediate portions. The chairs and clips are fastened down by fang bolts. The sleepers are of a mixed kind, some being rectangular and some being half round. The minimum size is said to be 4ft × 9in by 4½in. They are at an average distance of 3ft apart.

I do not consider the permanent way as well fitted for heavy Engines. I should have preferred to see rails with a flange laid upon wider sleepers, and bolted to these through the flange by fangbolts without the intervention of cast iron clips and chairs. The traffic will not however require I apprehend, that heavy Engines or high speed should be employed upon it.

The steepest gradient is 1 in 60. The sharpest curve near the Junction, has a radius of 9 chains. This must be traversed in all cases at only slow speed.

The embankments and cuttings have given a great deal of trouble in consequence of the nature of the soil and will require care and watchfulness for a long time to come. The greatest height of the works is 38 feet.

There are 5 Bridges under and 4 over the Railway besides a wooden viaduct 60 yards long. The woodwork of the Viaduct stands well under passing engines. The abutments have moved considerably from the weight of the bank behind them, but the buttresses which have been, or are being added for their support, appear to be well calculated to prevent further mischief. I have recommended that the wrought iron girders of a bridge at 2 miles 62 chains from the Junction near Chippenham should be strengthened and that cast iron girders of Lord Crewe's bridge [an occupation bridge between Hazeland Bridge and Black Dog. Known latterly as Mrs Coles' Bridge, it was between two fields belonging to Lord Crewe] should be replaced by others, as well as that the longitudinal beams which carry the rails over the other bridges should be connected by cross-ties and transoms. The sleepers require to be well packed up at the ends of the bridges and in one case at least, the longitudinal beams might be carried further back from the bridge with advantage.

The arrangements at Chippenham are not satisfactory. The Calne trains are intended to run in and out of the Great Western Station along the down main line. This cannot be avoided, apparently, without at least a partial reconstruction of the Station, but at all events the Signalman who protects the junction and the Signalman at the passenger platform should be provided with a good means of intercommunication.

At the Calne Station, the points which connect the sidings with the passenger line should be removed to a greater distance, and a safety switch should be added at the end of the sidings. A station signal is required near the points, and the distant signal should be removed to a greater distance from them, and provided with a better gallery for the use of the signalman, or a means of hoisting and lowering the signal lamp from below.

A proper approach to the station, and fencing round it are still required.

I have not yet received a Certificate as required to the working of the single line.

Pending the completion of the above requirements, I am of [the] opinion that the Calne railway cannot be opened without danger to the public using it.

I have etc.
H. Tyler
Capt Royal Engineers.

Lane was authorised by the Calne Railway directors to carry out the replacement of girders at Lord Crewe's Bridge, charging it to the Calne Railway account and deducting it from that of Hattersley. When these matters were corrected, T.L. Henly, chairman of the directors, had to travel 1,100 miles to find Tyler. He followed him to Dunta in Scotland, thence to Edinburgh and back to London, where he eventually caught up with him, the Calne Railway feeling the matter urgent, as lack of a certificate was delaying the opening. However, he failed to pass the railway on his second inspection:

To the Secretary of Trade                High Elms
   Whitehall                            Hampton Court
                                        7 October 1863
Sir,

I have the honor [sic] to report, for the information of the Lords of the Committee of Privy Council for Trade, that in compliance with the instruction contained in your minute of the second instant, I have re-inspected the Calne Railway.

I find that the wrought iron girders of the bridge at 2 miles 2 chains have been strengthened, and that the cast iron girders of Lord Crewe's bridge have been replaced by wrought iron girders. The new platform of the latter bridge, which is composed of rejected Barlow-rails, is not however so still as is desirable.

The longitudinal beams carrying the rails over the other bridges have been connected by transoms and cross-ties, and a new pair of wooden beams has in one case been supplied.

The points which connect the sidings with the passenger line at Calne have been removed to a quarter of the distance from the station, and a safety switch has been added at the head of the siding.

A station signal has been supplied near this point, and the distance [sic] signal has been moved to a suitable distance.

The fencing has been completed round the station, and an approach to the station has been partly constructed. An improved arrangement is, however, required for landing passengers, as I have pointed out on the spot, and a fence between the approach and the carriage-sheds.

The ballasting is still incomplete, as the Calne company has been unable as yet to obtain an Engine from the Great Western Company with which to finish it.

A hut is still required at Chippenham for the telegraph-instrument, by means of which the station and junction signalmen can be placed in continuous contact with one another. The system under which the latter has to work, stretches about 300 yards on one side and 120 yards on the other side of the line, ought to be improved, and his signal-handles should be brought to his hut.

More efficient gateposts are required at some of the level crossings, where the pillars, which are apt to be drawn out of the perpendicular, have been employed. The galleries of the Calne signals require to be improved and hand-rails should be supplied to the original ladders. Planking in the middle and at the sides of a culvert about two miles from Chippenham Junction should be supplied. A clock is wanting outside the station.

The Company has forwarded the enclosed certificate in regard to the working of the single line; but as they only undertake to *propose* to allow one Engine in Steam, or two or more coupled together to be at one time upon the single line, it is not a satisfactory one.

On these various accounts I am of the opinion that the opening of this branch would, by virtue of the incompleteness of the work be attended with danger to the public using it.

I have the honor to be
your obedient servant,
H.W. Tyler
Capt R. Engineers

Tyler made a third report:

The Secretary  
Board of Trade, Whitehall

High Elms  
Hampton Court  
27 October 1863

Sir,

With reference to my report of the 7th instant I have now the honor [sic] to enclose for the information of the Lords of the Committee of Privy Council for Trade, a letter from the Engineer of the Calne Railway stating that the requirements enumerated in that report have with one exception been completed. As regards the Chippenham Station of the Great Western Railway it appears that the telegraphic communication required has been established between the passenger platform and the hut of the signalman who works the junction signals, but that the handles of these signals have not been brought across to the hut as I recommended. The mode on which the Great Western points and signals are worked differs from that which has been adopted on narrow gauge lines and much improvement is needed generally on the broad gauge system. In the present, as in other instances, the difficulties alleged to stand in the way of the proposed alteration are, 1st, that the signals would not work so well as at present and 2nd that the signalman would not be so well able to perform his other duties if the alteration were effected. Under these circumstances I shall content myself with repeating the opinion I have already given as to the desirability of such an alteration and with leaving to the Great Western Company the responsibility of it, placing the signalman in charge of the junction on any duties in working switches at a distance from him which will interfere with his attention to the telegraph instruments.

I received a short time since from the Superintendent of the Great Western Company at Bristol, a copy of the regulations proposed for working this telegraph as well as that at the Bristol station. I note these regulations have been amended in accordance with my suggestions.

A satisfactory undertaking has now been received for the safe working of the single line, and regulations suggested by myself have also been put in force with an aim to it being properly carried out.

I am of [the] opinion that the Calne Railway may now be opened, subject to the foregoing remarks, with safety to the public.

I have etc  
H.W. Tyler  
Captain Royal Engineers

The total cost of constructing the line amounted to £49,283, plus £1,867 for the station buildings at Calne.

# CHAPTER TWO
# THE YEARS OF INDEPENDENCE

THE Calne Railway opened for goods traffic on 29th October 1863, the first train arriving at 8.30 a.m. laden with about 100 pigs and other goods. The opening to passengers was on Tuesday, 3rd November, which was declared a holiday at Calne. Shops were closed and the Band of the 4th Wilts Volunteer Corps in uniform paraded through the principal streets. At 10 a.m. they were met by 60 employees of Messrs G. & C. Harris who they escorted to the railway station, where a large number of people waited for the excursion to Bath which was to form the inaugural train. About 800 boarded it, but many more were left behind through lack of accommodation. All the employees of Messrs Harris, together with railwaymen at Calne, were treated by the firm to a 'sumptuous repast', Harris's also paying employees' excursion fares to Bath.

The railway directors gave a dinner at the White Hart Hotel to 60 guests. T.L. Henly, chairman, said that there was one toast which above all others deserved to be drunk, and that was the health of Mr Hattersley. He had found much of the money for them, 'where it had come from they knew not: he believed it had been begged, borrowed and obtained in every possible way short of stealing it (Hear, hear). Therefore if any man deserved thanks, it was Mr Hattersley, and as Mr Hattersley was not present, he would couple with that gentleman's health, the health of Mr Stephenson, who had represented Mr Hattersley in the construction of the line, and had, he was bound to say, always behaved towards the Directors most courteously and like an honest man (cheers).'

The Calne Railway directors wrote to the GWR saying that as the receipts of the excursion had greatly exceeded expectations, it was only fair that a mileage proportion of the whole receipts should be credited to their company. It is not known whether the GWR agreed.

Vandals are no modern phenomenon, for on 6th November it was discovered that a miscreant had placed two stones on the line opposite Keevil's Mill, west of Calne, immediately after the passing of the 11.15 a.m. up train. Fortunately, they were seen by H. Cooke, an engineer, and removed before any derailment occurred. A reward of five pounds was offered 'for the discovery of the perpetrators of this malicious act'.

Heavy rain in February and March 1864 caused many earth slips.

Surprisingly, the income of the Calne Turnpike Trust was little affected by the line's opening, figures being:

```
1862   £750  10  10
1863   £783   8   2
1864   £745   0   8
```

These figures showed very little variation until the end of the Trust in 1871.

In March 1864, H. Stallard, station master at Calne and formerly the Great Western Goods agent at Chippenham, complained that his work load was too heavy and that assistance was required. The Calne Railway directors failed to offer sympathy and observed that two clerks could do his work at a cost equal to that paid to him and asked the Great Western for his removal. The GWR replied saying that as the directors had asked specially for him to be appointed at Calne because they were impressed with his work at Chippenham, they could not agree to transferring him.

A. Mackintosh, GWR engineer, Worcester, reported on the line on 17th January 1865:

'Calne station: platform coping flush with wall leaving too great a space between carriages and it. Projecting nosing required. Station house in tolerably fair order. Goods shed small with 1 pillar crane. Wharf wall to cattle pen dry stone. Well with horse pump. Permanent way in 24ft lengths, 65lb/yd. In each length 8 sleepers, 6 rectangular and 2 half round. These last will all require to be turned over and be cut on top for rail. Nearly 3,000 sleepers to be so treated at cost of at least £100. Rails laid in small chairs which clip on one side of bottom flange, with iron wedge piece fitting in and clipping other flange, which is fanged through chair and wedge on to the sleeper. Intermediate chairs just have single iron clip on bottom flange, fanged down to sleeper. Last is weak, especially on curves. Ballast scant, and entirely of soft broken sand stone, fast working into dirt. 6ins of good gravel required. $\frac{3}{4}$ mile from Calne is $\frac{1}{4}$ mile long cutting. Slope on east side left for double line, and not trimmed or soiled. Requires draining. 2 miles from Calne is another cutting with slips, three men working on it. Bank at viaduct is weak. Already sent about 60 wagon loads of engine ashes to the place. Underbridges satisfactory – iron girders with timber decking. Brick abutments. Avon viaduct of timber with stone abutments, afterwards strengthened with stone buttresses. Overbridges have stone abutments with stone or brick arches. Fencing – rough posts with 7 wires and not of the very best. Quick [thorn] not planted.'

In 1863 a proposal was made to extend the Stonehouse & Nailsworth Railway (then in the planning stage and eventually opened on 1st February 1867) as the Gloucestershire & Wiltshire Railway to Christian Malford on the GWR main line to Bristol. Christian Malford was not the final objective, but on 5th July 1865 an Act, 28–9 Vic c.338, was passed for building the North & South Wiltshire Junction Railway from Christian Malford across downland to the Berks & Hants Extension Railway near Woodborough. The Wiltshire Railway, authorised by 28–9 Vic c.318 of 5th July 1865, was empowered to run from Pewsey, on the BHER a few miles east of Woodborough, over Salisbury Plain to Idmiston on the London & South Western Railway, six miles north-east of Salisbury. On 30th November 1865 a plan was published to extend the Calne Railway a mile from Calne station to link with the North & South Wilts Junction Railway which was to have run past Calne in a north-west/south-east direction. The plan never came to fruition as the main North & South Wilts Railway scheme proved abortive.

On 30th November 1872 a special meeting was called to consider the position in which the Calne company was placed in consequence of the secretary totally neglecting his duties. It was resolved that William Martin Vizard would no longer hold that office, Richard Clarkson being appointed at an annual salary of £20.

On 2nd June 1874 the Great Western offered to convert the Calne branch from broad to narrow gauge at cost. Conversion took place on 15th–16th August the same year, the line being opened for narrow gauge working on 17th August. The charge

11

of £500 was the only debt owed by the company to the GWR in March 1876.

## FINANCE IN THE EARLY DAYS
### Calne Railway Income October–December 1863, the first three months of opening

*October goods traffic*

| | | |
|---|---|---|
| Goods | 49 tons 13 cwt | |
| Cattle | 152 | Total receipts £ 13 10 0 |

*November*

| | | |
|---|---|---|
| Passengers | 3,918 | |
| Horses | 5 | |
| Dogs | 30 | £106 12 10 |
| Goods | 788 tons 5 cwt | |
| Cattle | 1,781 | £137 6 10 |
| Parcels | 584 | £6 9 8 |

*December*

| | | |
|---|---|---|
| Passengers | 2,685 | |
| Carriages | 1 | |
| Horses | 5 | |
| Dogs | 28 | £101 10 3 |

A little awkwardness arose between the company and Hattersley when a bill of £128 15s. 0d. was sent by the GWR for the hire of ballast engines in October and November, and a demand for £271 0s. 3d. for items required by the Board of Trade inspector. Disclaiming responsibility, he refused to pay for the ballast engines and, regarding the second bill, only reimbursed £150, saying that the directors had paid far too high a price for the work done.

The following June the Post Office offered to pay £25 annually for the conveyance of mail by ordinary trains. This was accepted and figured in the company's receipts for the half year to 31st December 1864, though from 1st October 1876, this source of income was reduced to £10 a year.

*Receipts. Half year to 31st December 1864:*

| | £ s d |
|---|---|
| Passengers | 654 16 11 |
| Goods & Cattle | 704 3 11 |
| Parcels | 27 17 5 |
| Mail & Sundries | 11 8 10 |
| | 1398 7 1 |

*Expenses* £ s d

| | |
|---|---|
| GWR working expenses | 855 2 8 |
| Maintenance of permanent way | 357 13 11 |
| Passenger duty, rates, etc | 131 19 5 |
| | 1344 16 0 |
| | 1344 16 0 |
| | 53 11 1 |

A profit of £53 11s. 1d. towards payment of debenture interest was hardly a success story, whilst the following half year to 30th June 1865 was little better, showing:

| | £ s d |
|---|---|
| Income | 1487 2 3 |
| Expenses | 1130 12 3 |
| | 356 10 0 |

The tonnage of goods carried was 5,067 compared with 4,775 for the same period in 1864.

An Act of 27–8 Vic c.16 of 28th April 1864 allowed the company to raise an additional £14,000 capital and £4,500 by borrowing. Unfortunately the company's minutes 1865 to 1869 are missing, so happenings in the intervening years are vague.

*Half year to 30th June 1869:*
11,569 passengers
4,489 parcels
6,179 tons of goods
9,734 cattle

In November 1869 it was agreed that 18s. 4d. per ton be charged on the carriage of dead pigs from Bruton to Calne instead of 23s. 4d. which had been complained of as too high a rate. The GWR said that the Calne Railway would receive 2s. 6d. instead of 3s. 4d. a ton. In December the Post Office applied to erect a telegraph line from Chippenham to Calne, offering a wayleave of £1 per mile and stating that the Calne Railway and GWR would be at liberty to erect wires on the poles set up by them.

Figures for the last half of 1869 showed an increase over that of the previous year except for passengers, the decrease in the latter partly accounted for by the greater number of excursion passengers carried in 1868, which included trains run for the Bowood Fete.

| Half year ended | Singles 1st 2nd 3rd | Returns 1st 2nd 3rd | Excursions 1st 2nd | Total |
|---|---|---|---|---|
| 31.12.68 | 567 4147 6227 | 207 2376 – | 18 1206 | 14,748 |
| 31.12.69 | 570 3870 6394 | 215 2168 – | 8 314 | 13,539 |
| Increase | 3 – 167 | 8 – – | – – | – |
| Decrease | – 277 – | – 208 – | 10 892 | 1,209 |

Parcel traffic improved from 4,708 to 4,811 items; traffic for coal, minerals and general merchandise increased by 608 tons and cattle from 8,724 to 9,548. Gross expenses of £1,026 in 1868 rose to £1,104 in 1869, bringing a revenue to the Calne Railway of £614. The line affected trade on the Wilts & Berks Canal as in 1865 only 335 tons of coal passed from Hanham, Bristol, to that waterway. The railway quoted 4s. 4d. a ton for carriage from Bristol to Calne whereas canal charges were as high as 5s.

At the directors' meeting on 21st December 1869 the Case & Opinion of A. Martineau, 15th October, was read.

'CASE: The Calne Railway was leased to the GWR at sufficient rent to pay the whole of the debenture interest plus a small margin of about £800 a year. In addition to the debenture debt they owe about £26,000 on Lloyds Bonds and debts of other creditors amount to about £2,000.

'All debentures are overdue and can be claimed for repayment. Lloyds Bondholders are passive. Two of the general creditors have attached the Company's surplus land by Writs of Elegit, but all parties are at present abstaining from active proceedings against the company.

'Advise directors whether they may without incurring personal liability, to censure appropriate the balance in hand in discharge of debts.

'OPINION: The debenture holders whose debentures have matured are entitled to file a bill for the appointment of a receiver of the future income of the line. As there is no receiver, he [A. Martineau] is of the opinion that the directors would incur no personal responsi-

## CALNE BRANCH——Passengers change at Chippenham.

**TRAINS FROM CALNE.**

| Fares, 1st class. | 2nd class. | 3rd class. | Starting from | Week Days. Ex. 1 & 2 class. | 1 & 2 class. | Ex. 1 & 2 | 1, 2, 3 class. | 1 & 2 class. | 1 & 2 class. | 1 & 2 class. | Distance from Calne. |
|---|---|---|---|---|---|---|---|---|---|---|---|
| | | | | a.m. | a.m. | a.m. | a.m. | p.m. | p.m. | p.m. | |
| . | . | . | **Calne** . dep. | 8 30 | 9 25 | 10 45 | 10 45 | 1 35 | 4 25 | 6 50 | 99¾ |
| 1/6 | 1/0 | 0/5¼ | CHIPPENHAM arr. | 8 45 | 9 35 | 11 0 | 11 0 | 1 50 | 4 40 | 7 10 | 5¼ |
| ... | ... | ... | CHIPPENHAM dep. | ... | 9 45 | 11 42 | 12 40 | 2 0 | 4 52 | 8 0 | 46 |
| 5/11 | 4/0 | 2/6 | BRISTOL . arr. | . | 10 40 | 12 25 | 2 0 | 2 50 | 5 40 | 9 5 | 80½ |
| .. | .. | .. | CHIPPENHAM dep. | .. | .. | 11 45 | 2 10 | 2 10 | .. | 7 25 | .. |
| 14/8 | 10/11 | 6/8½ | WEYMOUTH arr. | ... | ... | 2 30 | 5 20 | 5 20 | ... | 10 5 | 30¼ |
| 9/0 | 6/3 | 3/10 | SALISBURY arr. | . | . | 1 35 | 4 5 | 4 5 | . | 9 20 | . |
| .. | .. | .. | CHIPPENHAM dep. | 8 55 | .. | 11 12 | 1 0 | 3 42 | 5 25 | 8 33 | .. |
| 18/0 | 13/5 | 8/3½ | **Padding** arr. | 11 15 | ... | 2 40 | 5 45 | 6 10 | 9 0 | 11 5 | ... |

**TRAINS TO CALNE.**

| Fares, 1st class. | 2nd class. | 3rd class. | Starting from | Week Days. Ex. 1 & 2 class | 1 & 2 class. | 1, 2, 3 class. | Ex. 1 & 2 class. | | Ex. 1 & 2 class. | 1 & 2 class. | Ex. 1 & 2 class. |
|---|---|---|---|---|---|---|---|---|---|---|---|
| | | | | a.m. | a.m. | a.m. | a.m. | p.m. | a.m. | p.m. | p.m. |
| 18/0 | 13/5 | 8/3½ | **Padding** dep. | . | 6 0 | 7 5 | 9 15 | . | 11 45 | 2 0 | 4 50 |
| 1/6 | 1/0 | 0/5¼ | CHIPPENHAM arr. | .. | 9 45 | 12 35 | 11 40 | .. | 1 55 | 4 50 | 7 15 |
| 9/0 | 6/3 | 3/10 | SALISBURY dep. | 6 50 | ... | 10 25 | ... | ... | 1 40 | ... | 6 25 |
| 14/8 | 10/11 | 6/8½ | WEYMOUTH dep. | 6 0 | . | 9 0 | . | . | 12 50 | . | 5 20 |
| .. | .. | .. | CHIPPENHAM arr. | 8 45 | .. | 12 30 | .. | .. | 3 33 | .. | 8 25 |
| 5/11 | 4/0 | 2/6 | BRISTOL . dep. | 8 10 | ... | 11 30 | 12 15 | ... | 2 55 | 4 20 | 7 45 |
| . | . | . | CHIPPENHAM arr. | 8 53 | . | 12 40 | 12 53 | . | 3 38 | 5 20 | 8 30 |
| .. | .. | .. | CHIPPENHAM dep. | 9 0 | 9 50 | 1 0 | 1 0 | .. | 3 45 | 5 25 | 8 35 |
| ... | ... | ... | **Calne** .. arr. | 9 15 | 10 5 | 1 15 | 1 15 | ... | 4 0 | 5 40 | 8 50 |

**For Intermediate Stations between Bath and Bristol, Chippenham and London, Westbury and Salisbury, and Westbury and Weymouth, see pages 36 and 37.**

**1865 Timetable**

bility by appropriating the balance in hand to discharge any of the general debts of the company they may choose to select.'

In September 1870 the directors recommended that the GWR reduced the first and second class fares:

| | *From* | *To* |
|---|---|---|
| 1st single | 1s 6d | 1s 3d |
| 1st return | 2s 6d | 2s 0d |
| 2nd single | 1s 0d | 10d |
| 2nd return | 1s 6d | 1s 3d |

This was carried out on 1st April 1871, but the lower fare failed to encourage a sufficient number of extra passengers to cover the cost of the reduction.

| *Half year ended* | *Single 1st* | *2nd* | *3rd* | *Return 1st* | *2nd* | *Excursion 1st* | *2nd* | *Total* |
|---|---|---|---|---|---|---|---|---|
| 30.6.70 | 511 | 3309 | 6147 | 227 | 2073 | 4 | 67 | 12,338 |
| 30.6.71 | 542 | 3293 | 6239 | 231 | 2078 | 5 | 54 | 12,442 |
| Increase | 31 | – | 92 | 4 | 5 | 1 | – | 104 |
| Decrease | – | 16 | – | – | – | – | 13 | – |

Coal and mineral traffic carried increased from 2,361 to 3,001 tons; general merchandise from 3,583 to 4,333 tons and cattle from 13,664 to 17,052.

With the introduction of third class passengers to all trains in May 1872, the half year to 30th June saw the phenomenal rise in sales of third class singles to 9,572, an increase of 3,333.

*Analysis of ticket sales May/June*

| | *1871* | *1872* | *1871* | *1872* |
|---|---|---|---|---|
| 1st class | 423 | 383 | £ 31 2 6 | 28 18 6 |
| 2nd class | 3093 | 1697 | £154 16 11 | 84 17 2 |
| 3rd class | 3322 | 6831 | £ 76 2 2 | 156 10 8 |
| | 6838 | 8911 | 262 11 7 | 270 8 4 |

On 27th December 1873 the Great Western sent the Calne Railway a copy of a bill for the sale of the Calne line to the GWR. It pointed out that in 1869 the income was £1,227 and £1,717 in 1872 – an increase of just over £500 in three years. It observed that no interest had been paid on the paid up original shares.

Apart from the Parliamentary train, the Great Western raised its third class fare from 5½d to 7d on 1st June 1874. This had the effect of decreasing the number of third class passengers carried and increasing the number of second class.

A scheme of arrangement between the Calne Railway and its creditors was agreed on 17th March 1874. The whole of the share capital had been subscribed, but only 2,082 shares fully paid up; of course nothing had been paid on the contractor's 135 shares, while the remaining 1,283 shares on which nothing had been paid were forfeited. The company had borrowed £11,600 under mortgage and all interest on this had been paid up till February. The railway had cost more than anticipated and the company had incurred debts and liabilities which it was unable to pay. By its Act of 1864, the 1,283 forfeited shares were cancelled and the company authorised to issue new preference shares, and, in addition, up to £14,000 and, after issue, to raise £4,500 by mortgage. Unlike the action taken under the powers of 1860, no shares had been issued and no cash borrowed, so the company was unable to discharge its debts and liabilities. Bonds, or acknowledgements of debts under the company's seal, commonly called Lloyds Bonds, amounting to £23,510 and carrying an interest of five per cent, had been issued to the company by Hattersley.

Following complaints by Thomas Harris of high charges on the Calne Railway, H. Stallard, station master at Calne, wrote to Richard Clarkson, the Calne Railway secretary:

Great Western Railway
Calne Station
31 August 1875

Through Booking to Foreign Stations

Dear Sir,

Mr Hearne [District Goods Manager, Bristol] writes me as follows 'My opinion is that the system of invoicing to Chippenham only (of all through traffic) is an obstructive policy which prevents the Calne line being made available for other companies.

'There is no doubt that by accepting the Clearing House terminal, their allowance would not come to quite so much per ton; but this would I am convinced soon be more than met by increased traffic, through the line being thrown open and their rates etc put on a proper footing.'

I fully endorse Mr Hearne's views and may be permitted to add that this concession in the part of your Directors will stop numerous complaints from our Customers.

Truly Yours,
H. Stallard.

agreement signed 29th December that the Calne directors could undertake, subject to their shareholders' approval, to agree to the transfer of their undertaking to the GWR at any time before 1st January 1880, on receiving £20 of Great Western Consolidated Preference Stock for every £100 of Calne Ordinary Stock. This had been authorised by the Great Western Further Powers Act 37–8 Vic c 74 of 30th June 1874. This was one of the last meetings attended by Clarkson, as he died on 12th January 1878 after a few days' illness. The directors resolved to have H. Bevir, solicitor, act *pro tem.*, Edward

**December 1881 Timetable**

### Down Trains.            CALNE

**WEEK DAYS ONLY.**

| Distance | STATIONS | 1 Goods A.M. | 2 Pass. A.M. | 3 Pass. A.M. | 4 Pass. P.M. | 5 Pass. P.M. | 6 Pass. P.M. | 7 Pass. P.M. | 8 |
|---|---|---|---|---|---|---|---|---|---|
|  | Chippenham ...dep. | 6 45 | 8 35 | 10 0 | 12 35 | 2 20 | 5 20 | 8 10 | . |
| 4½ | Black Dog Sidg. „ | C R | C R | C R | C R | C R | C R | C R | .. |
| 5¾ | Calne ...........arr. | 7 0 | 8 50 | 10 15 | 12 50 | 2 35 | 5 40 | 8 25 | ... |

**Single Line, worked by Train Staff.**

On 17th September the directors resolved to accept the Clearing House terminal system as regards goods traffic.

| Half year ending | Single 1st | 2nd | 3rd | Return 1st | 2nd | Excursion 1st | 2nd | Total |
|---|---|---|---|---|---|---|---|---|
| 31.12.74 | 552 | 1356 | 16032 | 247 | 1302 | 9 | 1478 | 20,976 |
| 31.12.75 | 495 | 1422 | 16591 | 265 | 1779 | 9 | 1103 | 21,664 |
| Increase | – | 66 | 559 | 18 | 477 | – | – | 1,120 |
| Decrease | 57 | – | – | – | – | – | 375 | 432 |
|  |  |  |  |  |  | Net increase |  | 688 |

J. Hearne, district goods manager at Bristol, wrote to R. Clarkson, the Calne Railway's solicitor and secretary, on 21st March 1877, saying that the rate of carriage on pigs from Cork to Calne via Milford had been complained of as too high compared with the charges Bristol bacon curers paid from Ireland. Cork to Chippenham, 360 miles, was 4s 3d per head and Chippenham to Calne 5¼ miles at 3d per head, making a total from Cork to Calne of 4s 6d. He asked for a reduction on the Chippenham to Calne rate, but the directors replied saying that they did not feel justified in making a reduction.

The £31,320 debenture bonds became due on 1st January 1878 and interest on these was due to rise from four to five per cent if the bonds were not paid off on this date. Furthermore, this interest would have to be paid in perpetuity. As this amount of interest absorbed nearly all the company's earnings, the directors proposed asking the GWR to lend this sum in order that the bonds could be paid off. The Calne Railway in return was willing to ask that fresh arrangements be made between the two companies. To this end, R. Henly, chairman, and R. Clarkson, secretary, met Frederick George Saunders, the GWR secretary, at Paddington on 18th October 1877. The GWR being in a position to dictate terms, the outcome was an

R. Henly being appointed secretary on 22nd February at a salary of £30 a year.

On 17th December 1879 the directors considered a communication from the GWR calling on them to carry out the amalgamation agreed two years previously. However, the shareholders refused to ratify it, E.T. Clarkson believing it a mistake to sell to the GWR as he anticipated the branch becoming part of a through route to Marlborough. The shareholders said it was an 'inequitable and inadequate arrangement' and declined by a majority of 32 to sanction and confirm the agreement, forcing the directors to attempt to seek capital from another source. In March 1880 Saunders reminded the directors of their indebtedness to his company: the advantageous gauge conversion arrangements; the powers obtained in 1874 to sell out to the GWR; the assistance given in 1877 when the Calne Company was in difficulties over debenture capital. Saunders went on: 'The provisions in the Great Western Bill of the present Session were inserted upon the assumption that we were in friendly relations with the Calne Company.... The powers for vesting the Calne Company in the Great Western – Clause 63 – were inserted in order to give their effect to that Agreement.'

At the opening in November 1863 there were five passenger trains in each direction on weekdays. By August 1871 the timetable showed six trains each way taking 15 minutes for the 5½ miles. No separate goods trains were shown. In December 1881 the service started with a down goods 6.45 a.m. ex Chippenham, the engine working back on the first up passenger, whilst the up goods was worked at 8.35 p.m. ex Calne by the engine of the last down passenger. Most trains, including goods, were allowed 15 minutes, which remained the standard time for the trip right up to closure. All passenger trains called if required at Black Dog Siding, but goods trains only called in the down direction, which was odd, because the siding faced down trains.

Fortunately no serious accident occurred on the branch, mishaps being relatively minor. In February 1877 Colonel Yolland reported on an accident, attributing it to 'a young and inexperienced driver travelling at too high a rate of speed with an engine running the wrong end in front, and probably having one of its springs broken, over a portion of the line not in first-rate order'. He thought it was to be regretted 'that the railway company were not required, before the line was opened for traffic, to put down an engine turntable at Calne in accordance with the requirements of the Board of Trade, so as to avoid the necessity for running with the wrong end of the engine in front'.

The Great Blizzard of 1881 caused the train service to be cancelled on 18th January, running not being resumed until a goods train made its way through on the afternoon of the 20th. In the Great Blizzard ten years later, on 10th March, six empty wagons attached to the midday goods train from Calne were derailed by snow near Stanley Bridge and narrowly missed falling into the Wilts & Berks Canal. A breakdown gang from Swindon arrived in the afternoon, but the line was not cleared until the early hours of the following morning.

The Regulation of Railways Act, 1889, required the installation of block telegraph and interlocking of points and signals within two years, adding to the Calne Railway's financial burden. Although the 29th May 1862 lease had expired in 1873, the line continued to be worked on those terms, but on 17th March 1890 Henry Lambert, the Great Western's general manager, sent a letter proposing a new agreement on the following terms:

1. The Great Western to receive working expenses amounting to 55 per cent of the gross earnings.
2. The Calne Company to pay £150 per annum for the use of Chippenham station.
3. Interest on the £31,320 debentures to be reduced to 4½ per cent.

As a condition of this agreement, the Great Western directors stipulated:

1. Passenger accommodation at Calne must be improved, additional goods accommodation provided and interlocking of signals and points installed.
2. Accommodation at Black Dog siding improved, including locking.

The GWR was prepared to pay for additional accommodation at Chippenham, but the Calne company was required to pay rental.

On 7th April the Calne board replied asking that the agreement be for 21 years, that working expenses be 52½ per cent, with a £50 annual charge for the use of Chippenham station, and that the rate of interest on the debentures be 4 per cent. They could not see their way to paying for the enormous expense of block signalling. Lord Edward Fitzmaurice, a director unable to attend the meeting, wrote to his fellow directors saying that it was unjustifiable for them to declare a dividend of 5 per cent when such heavy expenditure was required to comply with Board of Trade regulations. He had consulted Paddington and found that estimated costs for the required improvements were £625 for Calne and £415 at Black Dog. He observed that the condition of Calne passenger and goods stations was disgraceful and that new stations should be built, for a total of £1,761 at Calne and £773 at Black Dog. He believed the dividend should not exceed 3½ per cent.

On 26th July 1890 the Calne Railway proposed terms for a new working agreement:

1. It to be on an annual basis, with six months' notice either side.
2. Working expenses to be 55 per cent of gross receipts.
3. The Calne company to pay £100 annually for the use of Chippenham station.
4. The debenture interest to be reduced to 4 per cent.
5. The Calne Railway to undertake the necessary works at Calne and Black Dog.

The GWR board refused to accept these proposals and on 20th November the Calne directors approved working expenses to be 55 per cent from 1st January 1891 instead of the 52½ per cent paid hitherto, a debenture interest of 4½ instead of 5 per cent, and £150 annual rent on Chippenham station.

On behalf of the GWR, Henry Lambert offered to purchase the Calne branch, the directors proposing to recommend this to their shareholders. In support they sent out a letter on 22nd January 1891 explaining details of the agreement and pointing out that improvements at Calne and Black Dog were estimated to cost considerably over £2,500. They said that the GWR had offered to purchase the Calne Railway at par, each shareholder to receive the amount originally paid on the share. Because of the decrease in income under the new working agreement, plus the heavy expenditure required on the stations, the directors recommended that the offer be accepted. At a meeting on 2nd February the proposal received 393 votes for and 158 against. To forward the take-over, the Calne board resigned and nominees of the GWR were elected in their stead, with Viscount Emlyn, chairman of the GWR, appointed chairman of the new Calne board. On 7 January 1892, Henly, the secretary who should have resigned, could not be contacted, but Albert E. Bolter took over his office on 20th January. Bolter became secretary of the GWR in 1910.

An Act of Parliament, 55–6 Vic c.233 of 28th June 1892 stipulated the amalgamation as official from 1st July that year. The GWR issued £13,117 Great Western Consolidated Ordinary Stock in exchange for Calne Railway shares amounting to £20,820.

*Calne Railway Capital*

| *Description of capital* | *Amount issued* £ | *Amount held by or on behalf of GW under statutory authority* | *Amount held by or on behalf of GW without statutory authority* | *Amounts held otherwise than by or on behalf of the GWR* |
|---|---|---|---|---|
| 5% deb. | 31,320 | 31,320 | – | – |
| 4% deb. | 11,600 | – | – | 11,600 |
| £10 shares | 20,820 | – | 20,820 | – |

This made a total capital of £63,740.

## CALNE BRANCH.

**Single Line, worked by Electric Train Staff.**

| Distances M. | Distances C. | DOWN TRAINS. STATIONS. | | Station No. | WEEK DAYS. 1 | 2 | 3 | 4 | 5 | 6 | 7 | 8 | 9 | 10 |
|---|---|---|---|---|---|---|---|---|---|---|---|---|---|---|
| | | | | | D | B | K | B | B | B | K | B | | B |
| | | | | | Em't M't'r | M't'r | Goods | M't'r | M't'r | M't'r | Goods | M't'r | Engi'e | M't'r |
| | | | | | | | | | | | | W | | |
| | | | | | A.M. | A.M. | A.M. | A.M. | A M. | P.M. | P.M. | P.M. | P.M. | P.M. |
| — | — | Chippenham .. .. | dep. | 1012 | 6† 0 | 7 0 | 8X13 | 8 55 | 10 24 | 12 20 | 1 55 | 2 20 | 3‖20 | 4 50 |
| 2 | 24 | Stanley Bridge Halt .. | ,, | 1151 | — | 7 6 | — | 9 1 | 10 30 | 12 26 | — | 2 26 | — | 4 56 |
| 4 | 45 | Black Dog Siding .. | ,, | 1152 | — | — | — | CR | CR | CR | — | CR | Y | CR |
| 5 | 44 | Calne .... .... .... | arr. | 1153 | 6†13 | 7 15 | 8 28 | 9 10 | 10 39 | 12 35 | 2 10 | 2 35 | 3‖35 | 5 5 |

| DOWN TRAINS. STATIONS. | | WEEK DAYS. 11 | 12 | 13 | 14 | 15 | 16 | 17 | 18 | 19 | SUNDAYS. 1 | 2 | 3 |
|---|---|---|---|---|---|---|---|---|---|---|---|---|---|
| | | B | | K | B | B | | B | B | | G | | K |
| | | M't'r | | Goods | M't'r | M't'r | | M't'r | M't'r | | Engi'e and Van. | | Goods |
| | | W | | | | | | SO | Z | | | | |
| | | P.M. | | P.M. | P.M. | P.M. | | P.M. | P.M. | | A.M. | | P.M. |
| Chippenham .... .... | dep. | 6 0 | .... | 7X30 | 7 50 | 9 12 | .... | *11 5* | *11 52* | .... | 6 40 | .... | 4 50 |
| Stanley Bridge Halt .. | ,, | 6 8 | .. | R | 7 56 | 9 17 | .. | *11 10* | *11 57* | .. | X | .. | — |
| Black Dog Siding .... | ,, | CR | .... | — | CR | CR | .... | — | — | .... | — | .... | — |
| Calne .. .. .. | arr. | 6 17 | .. | 7 45 | 8 5 | 9X27 | .. | *11 20* | *12 7* | .. | 6 55 | .. | 5 5 |

| UP TRAINS. STATIONS. | | WEEK DAYS. 1 | 2 | 3 | 4 | 5 | 6 | 7 | 8 | 9 | 10 | 11 | 12 |
|---|---|---|---|---|---|---|---|---|---|---|---|---|---|
| | | B | B | B | B | B | K | B | B | | B | K | |
| | | M't'r | M't'r | Motor | Motor | Motor | Goods. | M't'r | M't'r | Cat-tle. | M't'r | Goods. | |
| | | THO | | W | | | | | | | | | |
| | | A.M. | A.M. | A.M. | A.M. | A.M. | A.M. | P.M. | P.M. | P.M. | P.M. | P.M. | |
| Calne .... .... .... | dep. | *12 15* | 6 30 | 7 42 | 9 30 | 10 45 | 11 5 | 1 30 | 2 50 | 4 0 | 5 10 | 5 35 | .... |
| Black Dog Siding .. | ,, | — | — | CR | CR | CR | CR | CR | CR | Y | CR | — | .. |
| Stanley Bridge Halt .... | ,, | *12 24* | — | 7 55 | 9 39 | 10 54 | — | 1 40 | 2 59 | — | 5 19 | — | .... |
| Chippenham .. .. | arr. | *12 31* | 6 45 | 8 1 | 9 45 | 11 0 | 11 55 | 1 46 | 3 5 | 4 15 | 5 25 | 5 55 | .. |

| UP TRAINS. STATIONS. | | WEEK DAYS. 13 | 14 | 15 | 16 | 17 | 18 | 19 | 20 | 21 | SUNDAYS. 1 | 2 | 3 |
|---|---|---|---|---|---|---|---|---|---|---|---|---|---|
| | | B | B | B | | | B | | | | C | | B |
| | | Motor | M't'r | M't'r | Goods. | | M't'r | | | | Milk. | | Pass. |
| | | | | | | | SO | | | | | | |
| | | P.M. | P.M. | P.M. | P.M. | | P.M. | | | | A.M. | | P.M. |
| Calne .... .... .... | dep. | 7 0 | 8 15 | 9 35 | 9X45 | .... | *11 25* | .... | .... | .... | 7 40 | .... | 6 0 |
| Black Dog Siding .. | ,, | CR | CR | — | N | .. | — | .. | .. | .. | — | .. | CR |
| Stanley Bridge Halt .... | ,, | 7 10 | 8 23 | 9 43 | — | .... | *11 33* | .... | .... | .... | 7 42 | .... | 6 10 |
| Chippenham .. .. | arr. | 7X20 | 8 30 | 9 50 | 10 0 | .. | *11 40* | .. | .. | .. | 7 58 | .. | 6 18 |

X To convey Live Stock if necessary.
R Only runs when required to convey pig traffic to Calne.
N Only runs when 7.30 p.m. ex Chippenham runs.
W Time allowed. Stanley Bridge Halt for Milk and Milk Empties.
Y Runs on Calne Market Days only.
Z Wednesdays only.

**July 1914 Timetable**

CHAPTER THREE
# UNDER THE GREAT WESTERN

As early as October 1864 the directors of the Marlborough Railway linking that town with the Berks & Hants Extension Railway at Savernake, toyed with the idea of building an extension to Calne, but decided against it. The idea was resurrected in 1903 as the Central Wilts Light Railway, the chief promoters being Messrs C. & T. Harris, W.S. Butler (brewer, Marlborough), S. Darling (landowner, Beckhampton), and J. Horton (farmer and landowner at Winterbourne Bassett). Cecil Brown was the railway's engineer. The proposal was greeted with enthusiasm at Calne, people anticipating the development of new building sites and a demand for new houses, thus generally increasing the prosperity and trade of the town and the rateable value of property. A new line would have been of advantage to the town's staple industry – Messrs Harris's bacon factory – by improving the collection of pigs and distribution of bacon to the north and south of England via the Midland & South Western Junction Railway.

Although Calne and Marlborough were only $12\frac{3}{4}$ miles apart, since the stage coach service had ceased, the weekly carrier's cart had also stopped running, travel between the two towns by the circuitous rail route took between 2 hours 47 minutes to 3 hours 40 minutes. The return journey needed 3 hours 17 minutes to 4 hours, making it a good day's work to go from one town to the other and back. There was really only one way out of Calne in 1903 and that was via Chippenham. Promoters anticipated potential traffic from the vast corn-producing fields, thousands of sheep grazing on the Downs, and racehorse movements for trainers at Beckhampton. The line would also have opened up the stone circle at Avebury to tourists.

The estimated cost of the light railway, with a ruling gradient of 1 in 50, was £8,000–£9,000 per mile. A public meeting was held at the Town Hall, Calne, on 26th June 1903 for the purpose of passing a resolution in favour of the undertaking. The mayor presided and was supported on the platform by Mr Goddard, a solicitor to the promoters, Messrs J.M. Harris, W.S. Butler, H.G. Harris and G.I. Gough, town clerk. Among those present in the body of the hall were F.H. Henly, E.C. Henly and F. Ludgate, station master. The mayor said he had spoken to a great many people on the subject and not heard a single opposition raised, while the Town Council also gave the scheme its support. J.M. Harris reported that rumour had it that the Marquess of Lansdowne would probably object to the light railway, but Harris believed that any object for the good

'850' class 0–6–0ST No. 853 at Calne c.1905. The figure between the two shunters was station master Lloyd.
*Wilts Archaeological & Natural History Society*

Calne c.1908, the short platform canopy drawing attention to the parcels office extension to the new building. The GWR bus to Marlborough was a 20hp Milnes Daimler, fleet No. 31, registration AX 120. First registered as AM 533, it worked the Calne to Marlborough service at its inauguration before being sent to Abergavenny to open the service to Brecon when it was re-registered AX 120. From Abergavenny it was transferred to Cheltenham, Winchcombe and Bridgwater, finally returning to Marlborough in 1908.
*Author's Collection*

of Calne and its neighbourhood would receive his lordship's support. Cecil Brown, the line's engineer, had already mapped out the route of the scheme.

It was carefully pointed out that the line was not in opposition to the Great Western, the praises of Ludgate, GWR station master at Calne, being sung, and it was remarked that the light railway would be a feeder to both the Great Western and Midland & South Western Junction Railway. Principal tradesmen were much in favour of the light railway and farmers who would be served by it were without exception 'most liberal in their support'. Mr Goddard pointed out that it might not be known to everyone that milk at Waterloo was worth a penny a gallon more than at Paddington – a considerable sum to a farmer during the course of a year.

The plan deposited in May 1903 showed that the new line would be connected to the Great Western at the west end of the GWR layout at Calne station, the light railway's terminal passenger station being parallel with the main road and at right-angles to the GWR establishment. The new line would then have crossed Smelling's Hill by means of a tunnel under the road, passed under the Marquess of Lansdowne's drive and proceeded to Cherhill, keeping to the left of the main road which it crossed on the further side of Silbury Hill, following the course of the river Kennet until reaching Marlborough. Here one spur would have run to the GWR and another to the M&SWJR station. The line was to continue on to join the Berks & Hants Extension Railway two miles west of Hungerford. H.G. Harris said his firm had subscribed £200 towards applying for a Light Railway Order and he had personally subscribed £50. Unfortunately, the scheme fell at the first fence owing to the promoters being unable to satisfy the Light

A GWR bus from Marlborough turning into Station Road, Calne, c.1908.
*Author's Collection*

Steam railmotor No. 19 with an up train at Stanley Bridge Halte c.1905. The platform staging was later replaced with solid infill.
*Calne Town Council*

Railway Commissioners at the official enquiry regarding points of technical detail.

The directors of the GWR naturally kept a close eye on the Central Wilts railway scheme and when plans for the light railway were dropped, suggested running a bus between Marlborough and Calne. A trial run was made on Friday, 8th October 1904 with railway officials and the press as passengers. The vehicle was a 20 hp Milnes Daimler GWR No 29, registered AM 487, with a tare weight of 3 tons. It left Marlborough at 10.20 a.m. followed by a GWR charabanc previously used at Newquay and Slough, the newsmen opting to travel in the latter, which proved to be slower. Both buses arrived at Calne and, after a brief stay, returned to Marlborough, reaching it eighty minutes after departure. A celebratory luncheon was held at the Ailesbury Arms Hotel, the mayors of the respective towns joining railway officials including H.S. Kench, station master at Marlborough, and F. Ludgate, his counterpart at Calne. Two buses worked the service which started on Monday, 10th October, saved two hours over the rail journey and charged a single fare of 1s 6d compared with 3s 8d by rail. The timetable was:

|  | a.m. | p.m. | p.m. |
|---|---|---|---|
| Marlborough station depart | 8.45 | 1.30 | 5.25 |
| Calne station arrive | 10.10 | 2.52 | 6.50 |
| Calne station depart | 10.30 | 3.20 | 7.05 |
| Marlborough station arrive | 11.55 | 4.45 | 8.30 |

The GWR announced 'The motor omnibus will run, the condition of the roads permitting'. The first regular buses were No. 29 AM 487 and No. 31 AM 533.

The composite body provided seating for ten passengers inside, plus two beside the driver, whilst between the driver's back and the passenger section was a compartment for luggage, mail or goods. By means of flap seats, this area could alternatively be used to seat up to 8 passengers wishing to smoke. The vehicle had two brakes, one acting on the first intermediate gear shaft, and the other an expanding brake on the rear wheels, double acting and operated by pedal and ratchet. 20 hp Dennis bus GWR No. 158 was recorded working over the route in 1911.

The service was withdrawn after 30th September 1913, but later, with the threat of invasion of the area by the Bristol Tramways & Carriage Company, the Marlborough depot was reopened on 24th July 1924 and the Calne service worked by new 22 hp Chevrolets. From 11th July 1927 a through GWR bus service ran between Hungerford and Calne, from 25th August being extended to Newbury and Kingsclere daily, and to Aldermaston, Mortimer and Reading station on weekdays. From 1st June 1928 the Calne and Reading service terminated at Newbury. The service was cut back to Hungerford on 8th July 1929 and to Marlborough 22nd September 1930, finishing on 6th February 1932.

The introduction of a railmotor service to the Calne branch on 1st February 1905 was not welcomed by one letter writer to the *Devizes & Wilts Gazette*:

'I cannot refrain from raising what may be a feeble and ineffectual protest at the entire disappearance of the good and comfortable train service we have always enjoyed between Calne and Chippenham. This is now replaced by a single long motor omnibus having absolutely no first or second class, or smoking compartment, no racks

# GREAT WESTERN RAILWAY.

# RAIL MOTOR CAR
## ON
# CALNE BRANCH.
# Increased Service.

On and after WEDNESDAY, February 1st,

THE TRAINS BETWEEN

# CHIPPENHAM & CALNE

ON **WEEK-DAYS** WILL BE WORKED BY

## RAIL MOTOR CAR (one class only),

AT THE FOLLOWING TIMES:

|  |  | A.M. | A.M. | A.M. | P.M. | P.M. | P.M. | P.M. | P.M. | P.M. | P.M. |
|---|---|---|---|---|---|---|---|---|---|---|---|
| Chippenham | dep. | 7 10 | 8 45 | 10 23 | 12 40 | 2 17 | 4 22 | 6 0 | 6 55 | 8 22 | 10S27 |
| Calne | arr. | 7 25 | 9 0 | 10 38 | 12 55 | 2 32 | 4 37 | 6 15 | 7 10 | 8 37 | 10S42 |

|  |  | A.M. | A.M. | A.M. | P.M. | P.M. | P.M. | P.M. | P.M. | P.M. | P.M. |
|---|---|---|---|---|---|---|---|---|---|---|---|
| Calne | dep. | 7 45 | 9 25 | 10 45 | 1 15 | 3 20 | 5 10 | 6 25 | 7 12 | 9 30 | 10S45 |
| Chippenham | arr. | 8 0 | 9 40 | 11 0 | 1 30 | 3 35 | 5 25 | 6 40 | 7 25 | 9 45 | 11S 0 |

S Saturdays only.

## THE RAIL MOTOR CAR
WILL ALSO RUN AN ADDITIONAL TRIP FROM

# CHIPPENHAM TO BATH AND BACK

AS FOLLOWS:

|  |  | A.M. |  |  |  | P.M. |
|---|---|---|---|---|---|---|
| Chippenham | dep. | 11 25 | Bath | dep. | 12 5 |
|  |  |  | Box | ,, | 12 17 |
| Bath | arr. | 11 55 | Corsham | ,, | 12 27 |
|  |  |  | Chippenham | arr. | 12 37 |

The Wednesday trains leaving Chippenham for Bath at 9.50 p.m., and Bath for Chippenham at 11.0 p.m., will be worked by

**RAIL MOTOR CAR (one class only).**

**SMOKING.**—Passengers are respectfully requested to refrain from Smoking and Spitting in the Motor Cars.
**PUNCTUALITY.**—The Company have the greatest desire to make the Motor Car Service Punctual, and the public can very materially assist in that direction if they will be alert in getting in and out of the Cars.

Paddington, Jan., 1905.                **JAMES C. INGLIS**, General Manager.

(10,000 R. 8vo)        Arrowsmith, Printer, Quay Street, Bristol.        (B 109)

for light articles, very inefficient accommodation for luggage, and glass sides incapable of being opened, which will cause intolerable heat in summer. We have heard much about the convenience of the coming increased means of transport, but the motor runs each way only once more per day than did the trains. There have hitherto been eight trains out and in, and now the motor runs only nine times. No one would object to a motor in addition to trains for those who prefer third class and do not smoke, but they are not everybody.'

A Royal visit of Edward VII and Queen Alexandra to the Marquess of Lansdowne at Bowood in July 1907 caused alterations to the usual arrangements. To ensure smoothness of operations, the Royal Train made a trial run from Ladbrooke Bridge to Calne on 21st June. A special notice stipulated that the usual steam railmotor was to be replaced by a separate locomotive and train in order to cope with the additional passengers expected, and a run-round engine to be at Calne from 10.15 a.m. for as long as the train replaced the motor. The branch train was to be available to work extra trips if necessary. The notice stressed the importance of the 4.10 p.m. ex Calne being punctual, which, on arrival at Chippenham at 4.25 p.m., was to discharge its passengers at the west end of the down platform so that they could leave by the milk gate exit. The Royal Train arrived from Paddington at 4.40 p.m. on 20th July headed by No. 4006 *Red Star*, built only the previous April. Chippenham station was decorated with streamers and flags along the platform canopy, with flags flying over the exit. A portion of the booking hall was blanked off and transformed

A railmotor at Calne c.1910 after the track had been relaid with bullhead rail and the canopy extended in front of the new parcels office. The extension of the milk platform caused the engine release crossover to be moved further west.
*Collection Mrs. P. Gleed*

into a reception hall and decorated with the Royal Standard and the GWR coat of arms. Floral decorations in this hall had been carried out by Mr Gibson of Chippenham. Red poles and ornamental shields in the station yard helped to conceal its workaday appearance.

Steam railmotor No. 21 at Calne c.1905, with station master F. Ludgate on the left. This vertical matchboard-sided car first came into service in July 1904. The goods station canopy featured on the right was later removed. *Author's collection*

The original Black Bridge over the Avon.

National Railway Museum, York

**The replacement bridge shown shortly after construction in 1920.**  *National Railway Museum*

From Saturday until Monday the Royal Train was stabled at Swindon. On 22nd July, when the Royal party returned from Calne to Paddington, all milk churns were removed from the passenger platform at Calne by 10 a.m. and the public excluded after 10.45. The station was decorated with flags and bunting, there were the usual floral arrangements and the booking office floor was carpeted for the occasion. The formation of the Royal Train from Calne to Paddington was engine, brake van No. 1069, first class coach No. 8283, saloon No. 9002, royal saloon No. 9001, saloon No. 9003 and brake van No. 1070. Leaving Calne at 11.15 a.m., it arrived at Chippenham at 11.28, the branch engine being detached from one end and the London engine attached at the other. Its arrival time at Paddington was 1.15 p.m.

The timetable for April 1910 showed 12 trains each way, one class only, plus a late train on Wednesdays. The last train from Chippenham to Calne left as late as 11.50 p.m., being the continuation of the 11.15 ex Bath which allowed shop assistants (early closing at Chippenham and Calne on Wednesdays) to have an afternoon and evening in the Queen City of the West.

Calne branch permanent way gang, 1920, probably near Black Dog siding. They are from left to right: T. Baker, ganger R. Jefferies, J. Brittain, B. Brittain, R. Jones, C. Dobson, G. Robbins.
*Collection R. Jones*

# THE CALNE BRANCH

It returned from Calne at 12.15 a.m. – unusually late for a branch train. One up train ran on Sundays at 6 p.m. with no corresponding down working.

The railwaymen's strike caused the branch service to be suspended from 27th September until 5th October 1919. An emergency timetable was introduced a few days after the strike began, with a single departure from Chippenham being at 1 p.m., and from Calne at 11.45 a.m., 2 and 5 p.m. The normal service was again stopped by the 1926 strike.

The timetable for the summer of 1925 showed eight each way plus one each way mid-morning on the third Monday of the month for Calne cattle market, and a late train each Saturday evening. One train each way ran late on Sunday afternoons. An up train morning and evening was allowed 18 minutes to load milk churns at Stanley Bridge Halt, and one down evening train allowed 21 minutes to drop off the empty churns. An up milk train ran on Sunday mornings. Three goods trains were run on weekdays. In 1932 there were eleven trains each way on weekdays, plus a late train on Saturdays, and the monthly market train on the third Monday. Two trains ran each way on Sundays. The winter timetable for 1938–9 showed eleven trains each way, one down being mixed.

## CALNE BRANCH.

### Single Line, worked by Electric Train Staff.

**DOWN TRAINS — WEEK DAYS**

| Distance<br>M. C. | STATIONS. | Station No. | 1<br>Motor<br>A.M. | 2<br>Goods<br>A.M. | 3<br>Motor<br>A.M. | 4<br>Motor<br>A.M. | 5<br>M't'r<br>Y<br>A.M. | 6<br>Goods<br>A.M. | 7<br>Trow-<br>bridge<br>Motor<br>A.M. |
|---|---|---|---|---|---|---|---|---|---|
| — — | Chippenham dep. | 1042 | 6 25 | .. | 7 10 | .. | 8 55 | 10 23 | .. | 11 4 | 11 40 | .. | 11 55 |
| 2 24 | Stanley B. H'lt ,, | 1151 | 6 31 | .... | — | .... | 9 1 | 10 29 | .... | 11 10 | — | .... | 12 4 |
| 4 45 | Bl'k Dog Sid'g ,, | 1152 | — | .. | — | .... | CR | CR | .. | CR | — | .... | CR |
| 5 44 | Calne .... arr. | 1153 | 6 40 | .... | 7 25 | .... | 9 10 | 10 38 | .... | 11 19 | 11 52 | .... | 12 13 |

**DOWN TRAINS — WEEK DAYS—continued. / SUNDAYS.**

| STATIONS. | 8<br>Motor<br>P.M. | 9<br>Goods<br>P.M. | 10<br>Trow-<br>bridge<br>M't'r<br>P.M. | 11<br>Motor<br>W<br>P.M. | 12<br>Motor<br>P.M. | 13<br>Motor<br>P.M. | 1<br>Eng.<br>and<br>Van.<br>A.M. | 2<br>Motor<br>P.M. |
|---|---|---|---|---|---|---|---|---|
| Chippenham .. dep. | 2 0 | .. | 2 15 | 4 30 | 6 20 | 8 45 | 11 35 | .. | 10 0 | .. | 5 0 | .. |
| Stanley B. Halt ,, | 2 6 | .... | — | 4 36 | 6 32 | 8 51 | — | .... | X | .... | 5 6 | .... |
| Black Dog Siding ,, | CR | .. | CR | CR | CR | CR | SO | .. | .. | .. | CR | .... |
| Calne .... arr. | 2 15 | ... | 2 30 | 4 45 | 6 41 | 9 0 | 11 47 | .... | 10 15 | .... | 5 15 | .... |

**UP TRAINS — WEEK DAYS.**

| STATIONS. | Ruling Gradient 1 in | 1<br>Motor<br>W<br>A.M. | 2<br>Motor<br>A.M. | 3<br>Motor<br>A.M. | 4<br>Goods<br>A.M. | 5<br>Motor<br>Pass.<br>Y<br>A.M. | 6<br>Motor<br>P.M. | 7<br>Goods<br>P.M. |
|---|---|---|---|---|---|---|---|---|
| Calne .... .... dep. | — | 7 35 | .. | 9 20 | 10 45 | .. | 9 40 | 11 28 | .. | 12 37 | .. | 12 55 |
| Black Dog Siding ,, | 96 F | CR | .... | CR | CR | .... | 9 55 | — | .... | CR | .... | 1 9 |
| Stanley B. Halt .... ,, | 78 F | 7 47 | .... | 9 29 | 10 54 | .... | — | 11 51 | .... | 12 46 | .... | — |
| Chippenham .... arr. | 60 R | 7 53 | .... | 9 35 | 11 0 | .... | 10 10 | 11 57 | .... | 12 52 | .... | 1 25 |

**UP TRAINS — WEEK DAYS—continued. / SUNDAYS.**

| STATIONS. | 8<br>Motor<br>P.M. | 9<br>Motor<br>P.M. | 10<br>Goods<br>P.M. | 11<br>Motor<br>W<br>P.M. | 12<br>Motor<br>P.M. | 13<br>Motor<br>P.M. | 1<br>Milk.<br>A.M. | 2<br>Pass.<br>P.M. |
|---|---|---|---|---|---|---|---|---|
| Calne .. .. dep. | 2 40 | .. | 5 0 | 5 35 | 7 0 | 9 20 | 11†55 | .... | 10 45 | .... | 5 45 | .. |
| Black Dog Siding ,, | CR | .... | CR | — | CR | CR | SO | .... | — | .. | CR | .... |
| Stanley B. Halt .. ,, | 2 49 | .... | 5 9 | — | 7 12 | 9 29 | — | .... | 10 57 | .... | 5 57 | .... |
| Chippenham .... arr. | 2 57 | .... | 5 15 | 5 55 | 7 18 | 9 35 | 12† 7 | .... | 11 3 | .... | 6 3 | .... |

X To convey Live Stock if necessary.
W Time allowed at Stanley Bridge Halt for Milk and Milk Empties.
Y Runs on the third Monday in each month only.
Down Trains—Ruling Gradient 1 in 60 F. Stanley Bridge Halt, 78 R. Black Dog Siding, and 96 R. Calne. Black Dog Siding is worked as a Halt after passing of 5.10 p.m. Calne to Chippenham.

Timetable for 13th July to 20th September 1925.

Driver Johnny Dawes standing by GWR bus No. 1472, registration No. XV 5108, at Calne in 1930. Entering service on 12th December 1928, this 18-seater is on a Thornycroft A2 chassis.

*P. Vines*

GWR charabanc No. 1506, registration No. YU 1106, first licensed 4th April 1928. This view was taken in front of the Town Hall, Calne, in the summer of 1929 when the vehicle was allocated to Swindon. With a Maudslay ML3 chassis and Strachan body, this vehicle was eventually taken over by Bristol Tramways.

*Collection P. Q. Treloar*

## THE CALNE BRANCH

An extra train ran on the mornings of the first and third Monday each month, while a later train ran every Wednesday and Saturday. Three goods trains ran daily, plus an extra on Saturday evening. The Sunday service showed two passengers trains each way plus a down goods.

The timetable for 1944 was similar, giving twelve down and eleven up trains, plus an extra each way on Wednesdays and Saturdays. To cope with the increased number of RAF servicemen, four each way were run on Sundays.

Some turnround times were tight – the 5.20 p.m. ex Chippenham arrived Calne at 5.34, left again at 5.35 and arrived Chippenham 5.48, running non-stop in both directions. A turn round at Chippenham was allowed only 7 minutes, including crossing from the down main to the up bay.

1947 saw thirteen trains each way plus one on Wednesdays and two on Saturdays. Four ran each way on Sundays.

An unidentified Dean Goods with an engineers train, laying water pipes to serve Messrs. Harris's factory c.1932. The work was carried out by Blackford & Son. *D. G. Blackford*

The Harris's pipe-laying train c.1932. *D. G. Blackford*

# CHAPTER FOUR
# ALONG THE ROUTE

Chippenham station, looking east on 6th June 1951, with the down main on the right, the Weymouth bay platform on the left, and the up main on the far left.
*L. B. Lapper*

CHIPPENHAM station opened on 31st May 1841, the Brunel-designed single-storey station in Bath stone having a low pitched roof forming a platform canopy. The principal buildings are on what was the down platform. Concurrent with the opening of extensions to Salisbury and Weymouth in 1856–7, the station was considerably enlarged by the Chippenham railway contractor, Rowland Brotherhood, to cope with its junction status. A down bay and train shed were built, covering the down platform and island platform. An unusual feature of the shed was that by 1898 its ends differed, that at the east being closed in above train roof level, a glass draught screen shielding part of the platform, while the west end of the shed was completely open. The main line was diverted towards the new booking offices slightly nearer the town and new locomotive and good sheds were built at the same time, all this work being completed by mid-1858. Later an up bay was made to cope with the opening of the branch to Calne and in 1900 the layout was further modified when the Weymouth bay was turned into a through road, the overall roof being removed c1905. Opposite ends of the platform were controlled by different boxes, so to avoid special permissive block working, this through line later had back-to-back buffer stops erected, dividing it into a Weymouth bay and a siding known as the New-Found-Out. Platform 1 was the down main, No. 2 the Westbury and Weymouth bay, No. 3 the up main, and No. 4 the Calne bay. In 1946 the GWR drew up plans for a passimeter booking office, though this never came to fruition. With dieselisation the New-Found-Out became redundant and was removed on 23rd April 1964, the Weymouth bay being lifted on 21st August 1966. On 1st February 1976 the down main line was slewed over to the south side of the island platform in preparation for HSTs. Today the single-storey, slated roof, Bath stone station is a Grade 2 listed building, the main offices adjoining what was the down platform. Further west a public footbridge crosses the station platforms. Originally lattice girders throughout, those on the southern half were replaced by plate girders in 1955, the remainder being renewed with welded open girders about two years later. By private arrangement during World War 2, Tom Smith, an engine driver who lived at Station House, stored bicycles for servicemen, making a charge of sixpence a day or a shilling for weekends, the income being donated to charity. After the war quite extensive bicycle storage sheds were built on the down platform.

Near the main entrance to the station, which still has a Barlow rail forming a gatepost, was the station master's house, stables, garage and six railwaymen's cottages built of Bath stone, one occupied by a railway policeman. The derelict

27

Chippenham c.1898 with a crowd waiting to board a down train entering the station. *Yelde Hall Museum Chippenham*

'2201' class 2–4–0 No. 2218, built 1882 at Chippenham, with an up stopping train c.1905.
*Yelde Hall Museum Chippenham*

# ALONG THE ROUTE

Calne Junction, c.1900, with the Evans O'Donnell & Co. signalling works in centre background. The slotted signals were worked from Chippenham No. 1 signal box on the down side of the line; this was later replaced by Chippenham East box. The accommodation bridge under the Calne branch was known as the Devil's Arch. *Author's Collection*

stables were rehabilitated during World War 2 when two cart horses were re-introduced. The road vehicle maintenance depot shared the same building and Thornycroft goods lorries normally kept in the goods yard were taken to the ex-stables for repair. Each morning drivers collected their horses from the stables and made for the goods shed where they collected their carts. The horses were used for delivery in Chippenham, the motor lorries for Chippenham and its environs, and a Morris Commercial motor express cartage van, with sliding doors to the cab, was used for parcels delivery from the parcels office. GWR motor lorries first appeared in Chippenham about 1918, and by 1924 solid tyre AEC and Thornycroft vehicles were in use. They delivered to Castle Combe, Colerne, Dauntsey, Luckington, Lyneham and Yatton Keynell. In 1939 a mechanical horse with about eight trailers was used for town deliveries, later replaced by two 6-tonners. The Westinghouse Brake & Signal Company were good customers, one GWR vehicle being kept busy shuttling between works and station with small packages, only large items using the works siding. Nestlés milk factory also kept a GWR horse and cart or motor lorry busy. Milk was collected from farms by a GWR AEC lorry. There were about six lorry drivers and two horse drivers.

The stone-walled, two-road goods shed, 194ft in length, contained three 2-ton cranes. At its west end were workshops for permanent way carpenters, painters and plumbers. The GWR carpenters' lean-to shop was demolished circa 1947 when the goods shed was modified so that Royal Navy trailers from Hawthorn could be backed at right-angles to the loading platform. The shop was used by maintenance 'chippy' Percy Scott ('Scottie the chippy') and his mate. The goods shed was dismantled circa 1976, its site being used to extend the station car park.

When transferring cattle feed from wagon to the two GWR warehouses situated on the up side of the line, strong planks and trestles were used to link wagon with warehouse, the material being transferred in two-wheel sack trucks.

Between the goods shed and the station entrance in Cocklebury Road was a milk shed, open on one side for lorry access. Apart from loading Nestlés milk for Brentford Dock, ten vans leaving nightly, it was used for unloading tinplate for Nestlés factory. The trailer was left for the contents to be loaded into a railway van and an empty trailer taken back. Bags of sugar were also taken to Nestlés and timber for making boxes in which to pack the cans.

In the booking office were three single needle telegraph machines for railway use: the Swindon-Bristol circuit; Chippenham-Taunton and Chippenham-Westbury. A telephone, in a kiosk for privacy, stood in the corner of the booking office so that telegrams could be sent on behalf of the public, messages being phoned through to the General Post Office at Chippenham.

The station gave rise to considerable industry – on the up side were a foundry, brewery, cheese factory, bacon factory, signalling works and gas works as well as coal, salt and hay merchants, and on the down side was a stone works.

Chippenham was exceedingly busy during World War 2 because, apart from the needs of the town and its environs, there were ammunition dumps, RAF camps and a Royal Naval

A 2–4–0T entering Chippenham with an up stopping train c.1914. The Dunkerton Colliery wagon near the GWR warehouse came from the newly extended Camerton branch.
*Author's Collection*

An open cab tank engine with its tanks being replenished alongside the down main platform. In the foreground, coal from a Radstock Coal Company's wagon is being transferred to F. C. Mortimore's lorry.
*Yelde Hall Museum, Chippenham*

# ALONG THE ROUTE

Up side goods yard and Mortimore's coal sidings as seen from the footbridge c.1930. Former Brotherhood's works are on the left.
*Author's Collection*

depot in the surrounding area. Ten vanloads of stores for the RN Depot, Copenacre, left daily; they were classified Priority A and sent away on the first passenger train. On one occasion Warflats were put in the fish dock and end-loaded with Army tanks. The 4.30 a.m. Swindon to Weymouth parcels train arrived at Chippenham at 5 a.m. and there was always a race to see if the station staff could get it away before 6 a.m. Following its departure, the platform was stacked with parcels, vegetables, hundreds of nets of sprouts for RAF camps, fruit, fish and Lyons' cakes measuring about $2\frac{1}{2}$ ft by $1\frac{1}{2}$ ft nicknamed 'blockbusters' after a World War 2 bomb. Red insulated boxes of Lyons' ice cream were also consigned to the camps from

Chippenham down platform in 1906 after the train shed had been replaced by a platform canopy. The view shows former Weymouth bay on the left, as a through road.
*Yelde Hall Museum, Chippenham*

## THE CALNE BRANCH

Looking west from Chippenham station, Easter 1937.  *M. J. Tozer*

An up stopping train arriving behind 'Bulldog' class 4–4–0 No. 3306 *Armorel*, Easter 1937. *Armorel* was the first 'Duke' to be rebuilt as a 'Bulldog'.
*M. J. Tozer*

**Looking west through Chippenham station, Easter 1937.**   *M. J. Tozer*

Kensington Olympia. When the 6.35 a.m. from Calne arrived at Chippenham, porters filled the luggage compartments of the two auto trailers.

The present permanent way office near the station entrance, a Grade 2 listed building, is believed to have been Brunel's site office. Its shape led it to be called the 'knife box'. Later it became a refreshment room, unusual because, as it was off the platform, a travel ticket had to be shown at the barrier in order to patronise it. Because of its situation, it was also used by non-railway travellers. After closure as a refreshment room, it was hired for dances and whist drives. Pre-1939, refreshment room staff travelled from Swindon, locals not being employed in the rooms except as cleaners. During World War 2 the building was used as a hostel for refreshment room staff. The main refreshment room was on the down platform, the one on the up platform not always being open. It is said that the refresh-

**Enamel sign at Chippenham station.**   *P. Q. Treloar*

ment room staff tended to come from unhappy homes and were therefore glad to live away in a hostel. After the war the building was used as a store and then let to the GPO.

Weekly Staff at Chippenham in 1898 consisted of 2 passenger guards, 1 branch guard, 4 goods guards, brakesman, 4 relief-men, 10 signalmen, 2 policemen, 2 foremen, 1 parcels porter, 1 luggage stower and 1 shunter. The branch guard became a rail motor conductor in February 1905. In 1904, due to increased work in the goods department, the passenger and goods departments, hitherto under control of the station master, were placed in charge of W. Wells, the duties of station master being continued by Mr Philips.

Staff at Chippenham at 20th November 1920 consisted of station master, 1 chief clerk, 1 parcels clerk, 2 booking clerks, 1 woman booking clerk, 4 passenger guards, 3 goods guards, 4 goods shunters class 2, 3 goods shunters class 4, 2 passenger shunters, 12 signalmen, 1 signal lampman, 3 ticket collectors, 2 passenger foremen, 4 parcels porters, 1 porter/guard, 7 porters, 1 waiting room attendant (woman).

An official report of 20th November 1920 stated:

> 'Traffic consists of farm produce and is very heavy, showing a considerable increase over pre war figures and maintaining heavy advances, especially in connection with milk traffic. Parcels transfer work is considerable. 5 clerks employed and fully occupied in booking, parcels and telegraph work. Postal messages dealt with 9 a.m.–7 p.m. and the average daily messages (railway and postal included) are approximately 60.

> 'A class 2 shunter is in charge of shunting operations at all times. This new working brought in on Monday last (16th November) – meaning class 2 in charge. Three class 2 men cover 24 hours and the fourth works 5 p.m. to 1 a.m. relieving the passenger foreman from 11 p.m. to the arrival of the midnight ex Paddington which arrives Chippenham 2.29 a.m.

> '2 passenger shunters employed and necessary to deal with the shunting of passenger train vehicles between 6 a.m. and 10 p.m. Any shunting after 10 p.m. performed by passenger porter on duty. 3 signalmen employed for Langley Crossing box. Up and down refuge sidings at Langley Crossing frequently used as Christian Malford box is switched out 4 p.m.–8 p.m.

> '3 ticket collectors over 24 hours and these men give relief in the ticket office 6–8.30 a.m. and 9.30 p.m. till the departure of the last down train at 2.29 a.m. The collector on the 10 p.m.–6 a.m. duty remains in charge after the departure of the 2.29, being available to advise the Callman in case of fogs arising, or to obtain assistance in the event of any emergency.

> 'The 7 porters in addition to their ordinary work:
> Light up Lacock halt 1.50 p.m.–4.0 p.m.
> Stanley Bridge halt 2.15 p.m.–3.0 p.m.
> Unload milk empties Stanley halt 11.35 a.m.–1.15 p.m.'

There were four goods guards at Chippenham in 1959 with three 20-ton vans and one of 16 tons, the latter being kept as spare.

After the war Chippenham railwaymen formed their own football team, the Railway Ramblers, playing at Cocklebury on a field almost opposite Chippenham East box, the site now

**Some of Messrs. Harris's branded vans standing alongside milepost 94, on the up side of Chippenham station, 1937.** *M. J. Tozer*

Looking east through Chippenham station, Easter 1937. *M. J. Tozer*

The water tank supplied by a pump at Fogamshire, fed the water columns and the station's non-drinking water taps. Mortimore's coal yard is in the foreground. *D. J. Hyde*

Chippenham station, looking west, Easter 1937. The auto coach and gas cylinder wagon are standing in the New-found-out Siding, the 0–4–2T and van in the Fish Dock, and coach and vans in the parcel dock.
*M. J. Tozer*

The down main platform is on the left of this 1951 view. The Weymouth bay is on the right and the New-found-out siding on the far right. The windows on the right illuminated the refreshment room on the up platform.
*L. B. Lapper*

# ALONG THE ROUTE

Chippenham, looking towards Paddington, Easter 1937. The brake van on the left is branded 'Chippenham'. *M. J. Tozer*

The west end of Chippenham goods shed with part of the Nestlés shed on the right. The notice warned 'Beware! Shunting operations. Look both ways.' *D. J. Hyde*

Left: The partly open shed was used for the receipt of tinplate for Nestlés and loading filled tins of milk for forwarding to Brentford Dock. Fenner's coal yard is on the left. *D. J. Hyde*

0—4—2T No. 1446 propelling auto trailer W77W with the 1.7 p.m. from Calne past Chippenham goods shed on 13th March 1955.
*Hugh Ballantyne*

Fenner's coal yard, and Wilts United Dairies.
*D. J. Hyde*

The goods shed in May 1968.  *D. J. Hyde*

This view, taken in the summer of 1967, shows the lean-to goods office and corrugated iron wartime extension.  *R. Ball*

Albert Ball looking out of Chippenham East signal box on 17th July 1953. The shed to the right was used for lamp oil.  *R. Ball*

Signalman Albert Ball at the frame of Chippenham East signal box on 17th July 1953. The special train notices were pinned above the fireplace on the right. Also on the right are the signalmen's lockers, a telephone, and token instrument for Chippenham East–Calne. The coal scuttle and stove can also be seen. The lever collar on the left was being used for holding a boiled egg! The megaphone to the left of the signalman's head, was used for giving instructions to footplate crews or shunters.  *R. Ball*

The 5.35 p.m. Calne–Chippenham auto setting down the token at Chippenham East signal box on 17th July 1953. The fireman on the engine had the tablet whilst the guard in the doorway of the auto car had a document for signalman Albert Ball.   *R. Ball*

Driver Bernard Baker handing the tablet to signalman Robert Jones at Chippenham East signal box c.1951. Unusually, the '14XX' class 0–4–2T is at the Chippenham end of the train, perhaps because it didn't have a passed fireman officially required for auto working, and therefore had to be run round at Calne. The tall chimney belonged to the Wilts United Dairies.   *R. Jones*

Driver's view of Chippenham East signal box, 19th August 1964. The DMU is just about to join the down main line. The hut on the right was the signal lineman's, whilst the four trucks were stabled on the Westinghouse siding. The setting down post for the token was between the up and down main lines.　*D. Pritchard*

The view from Chippenham East signal box c.1958 with the turntable and loco shed on the left.　*M. B. Sadler*

# ALONG THE ROUTE

Chippenham East with the up main line in the centre of the picture and the Calne branch diverging to the right. *R. Ball*

An 0–6–0PT propelling the 5.35 p.m. Calne–Westbury auto past Chippenham East inner home, c.1953, with one of Harris's vans behind the engine. *R. Ball*

44 THE CALNE BRANCH

Calne Junction c.1960, shortly after the arms of the up branch inner home had been placed lower down the post. *M. B. Sadler*

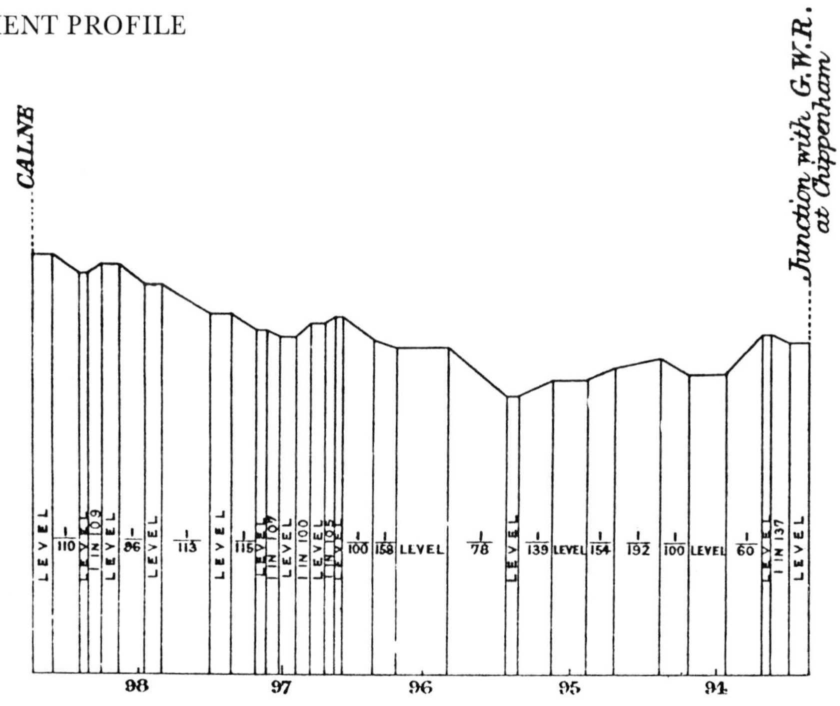

# ALONG THE ROUTE

0—4—2T No. 1446 with auto trailer No. W90W, on the 12.20 p.m. Calne—Chippenham, approaching Calne Junction on 7th June 1954.
*R. E. Toop*

part of the present cattle market. The pilot engine stood on a siding overlooking the field and sounded a fanfare of whistles each time the Ramblers scored. Chippenham men passing on local trains also blew whistles of encouragement, the signalman at Chippenham East cheering them on through his megaphone, normally used for shouting instructions to drivers.

Until the present cattle market was built on Cocklebury field, it was held in the centre of Chippenham. Market day was Friday and cattle would be driven through the streets to the cattle pens on the London side of the goods shed. This was a scene of intense activity and cattle trucks would be attached to the rear of passenger trains. The 5 p.m. Chippenham to Bristol East Depot goods, worked by a St Philip's Marsh crew, ran as a pick up goods every day, but on Fridays it was uprated to a non-stop vacuum fitted goods comprised mainly of cattle trucks. The engine allocated for this train was anything from a 'Hall' to a pannier tank.

Leaving Chippenham, a branch train passed Chippenham East signal box and, when parallel with the turntable, curved south-east to the single line branch at Calne Junction. Here a notice stated that no blue or red engine was allowed beyond the board. The line rose and passed through a cutting and under a round arch bridge typical of the branch, and arrived at Black Bridge over the Avon. Originally of timber, it was replaced by a steel structure in 1920, the main girders travelling from Horseley Company's Tipton, Staffordshire works on 1st August 1920 via Birmingham and Oxford. Their lengths were 105ft 11in and 80ft 11½in respectively, the weight of the largest girder being 29 tons. The *Great Western Railway Magazine* of 1921, page 111, carried a description.

**Chippenham East fixed distant signal.** *R. Jones*

# 46 THE CALNE BRANCH

0—4—2T No. 1446 with auto trailer No. W90W on the 11.48 a.m. Chippenham to Calne (11.10 a.m. ex Trowbridge), passing under Cocklebury Bridge shortly after leaving the junction. The gradient changed from 1 in 137 up, to 1 in 60 down. 7th June 1954.
*R. E. Toop*

The abutments and brick central pier on the east bank still stand. These are the stone originals, reinforced with engineer's brick when the replacement bridge was built. The deck was about 30 feet above river level. Few earthworks were required, the line following the gentle undulations of the almost flat country. Immediately before Stanley Bridge halt the gradient changed from 1 in 139 down to 1 in 80 up.

## STANLEY BRIDGE HALT

In March 1888 F.H. Goldney said that if the Calne Railway would make a station at Stanley Cross Roads, Sir Gabriel Goldney would find the whole of the money required and consent to be repaid by receiving half the gross takings at the station. The GWR engineer prepared an estimate for constructing a passenger and goods station at Hazeland Bridge, a mile nearer Calne, and this would have served Stanley. His estimates were:

| | |
|---|---|
| Passenger station and locking | £680 |
| Goods siding, locking and cartway | £976. |

It was decided not to proceed with this project, nor that at Stanley, the terms offered for the latter not being practicable.

The halt, 2 miles 4 chains from the junction, was opened on 3rd April 1905 following the inauguration in February that year of a steam railcar service. Situated on the west side of the track, shrubs were planted opposite. The platform was an earth bank held in place by a sleeper wall and topped with gravel. A corrugated iron pagoda was provided to shelter waiting passengers and beyond was a timber-built milk shed called 'the shed with the hole at the back', strangers being inquisitive about the small gap where churns were put through. Behind the halt was a space for milk carts which queued up to unload, these coming from Tytherington and Bremhill as well as from around Stanley. Milk traffic grew to such an extent that a porter from Chippenham had to be sent to help the guard load the milk in the evening, and sometimes it took a quarter of an hour at midday to offload the empty churns.

Wiltshire Farmers Limited, Chippenham, sent whey in very old churns to pig farmers at Stanley Bridge for use as pig feed. The churns were apparently so old that they appeared unhygienic even for pigs. The whey travelled on the midday mixed train from Chippenham, and a Calne porter went to Chippenham on the 10.50 a.m. to help unload at Stanley Bridge. It was not a popular job because if any whey was split on a uniform it was difficult to remove and stank.

# ALONG THE ROUTE

Black Bridge carrying the line across the Avon. This view was taken looking upstream.  *National Railway Museum*

Stanley Bridge Halt, looking towards Calne.  *G. Beale*

The same train leaving Stanley Bridge Halt. *M. E. J. Deane*

Looking down onto Stanley Bridge Halt c.1951. *M. E. J. Deane*

DMU driver's view of the approach to Stanley Bridge Halt en route to Chippenham. The post and wire fence to the left has replaced the gap left by the removal of 'the shed with the hole at the back'.  *D. Pritchard*

The milk shed became redundant and was removed circa 1947–8, a ganger remembering catching a rabbit from under it when it was being demolished. Where the milk shed had been, a post and wire fence protected passengers from wandering off the back of the platform, this contrasting with the post and rail elsewhere.

The halt was unstaffed, coming under the auspices of the Chippenham station master. From the week ending 1st February 1909, parcels were handled by an agent. Although at first a porter was sent from Chippenham to light the three platform lamps, plus the one in the waiting shelter, this proved uneconomic and latterly the lamp man filled them about twice a week in the iron lamp hut beyond the platform ramp and they were turned on at twilight by the train crew. The attractive copper lamps were sawn off and stolen shortly before closure. A lad porter from Chippenham went to Stanley Bridge halt once a week to brush out the waiting shelter, but not the milk shed.

In fields by the site of the halt, GWR boundary posts can still be seen, dated 1889 on the north-east side and 1885 and 1900 on the south-east.

The line climbed at 1 in 80 from the halt and rose on an embankment to cross the Wilts & Berks Canal. The bridge itself was filled in circa 1934 and today the canal in the vicinity

Crewed by Bath men, 2–6–2T No. 5523 climbing the gradient of 1 in 80 away from Stanley Bridge Halt with the 10.22 a.m. from Chippenham on 25th October 1955.  *Author*

Collett 0–4–2T No. 1433 near Hazeland Bridge with the 12.54 p.m. to Calne, on 25th October 1955. *Author*

is very overgrown. To the east are the remains of Stanley Abbey, founded by the Cistercians in 1154. The line passed through Great Bodnage Copse, under Hazeland Bridge, through Searchers Wood and passed Calne Corporation's Sewage Farm, Black Dog Halt, crossing the A4 immediately before Black Dog halt.

## BLACK DOG HALT

This private station, 4 miles 28 chains from the junction, was situated on the edge of the Marquess of Lansdowne's Bowood Estate. In February 1864, and again in August 1869, the Marquess of Lansdowne's agent wrote to the Calne Railway directors asking for a siding to enable him to unload coal and other heavy goods for the Estate. In August 1870 it was agreed that the £300 cost of making a siding would be returned to him by rebate of 20 per cent on his carriage account. The Marquess would pay the same rates from the siding as he would have paid from Calne station, and parcels and goods would be delivered or collected once daily. That same year the cost of erecting a temporary platform for the Bowood Fete cost the company £4 10s. 0d. At the directors' meeting on 19th September 1873 it was announced that Black Dog Siding was complete and it was hoped would be shortly opened. On 22nd April 1875 Colonel Rich reported for the Board of Trade on the re-inspection of the siding and found that a clear view of the down distant signal was obscured by an intervening tree; a home signal required either moving, or the provision of a repeating signal, and points required adjusting. The siding was first mentioned in the working timetable for June 1875.

At a personal cost of £598 3s. 10d. Lansdowne provided a house bearing his family crest in which the station master lived rent free, additionally paying part of his wages and providing him with four tons of coal annually. In return the railway company agreed to make no appointment without first obtaining His Lordship's permission, prospective members of staff being first interviewed by him. The arrangement was detailed in a memorandum.

Great Western Railway
Divisional Superintendent's Office
Bristol
April 20 1875.

**Black Dog Siding near Calne**
A man to be appointed by the Great Western Railway to take charge of the siding – light the lamps, give signals, collect tickets (when necessary), book parcels and do all the work the G.W. may require of him and that in addition he shall look after Lord Lansdowne's stores – coals – and any other work that may be required of him at the Station consistent with his first duty to the Company, and that he should be paid 20s per week besides being found a house and coal by Lord Lansdowne. That, in addition to finding the house and coal, Lord Lansdowne will pay a sum of 8s weekly towards the man's pay, the G.W. paying the difference of 12s and finding clothes and the ordinary stores for working the Station, signals etc. Six months'

No. 1433, again near Hazeland Bridge, with the 1.12 p.m. ex Calne on 25th October 1955. *Author*

Lord Crewe's bridge from the south. *Author*

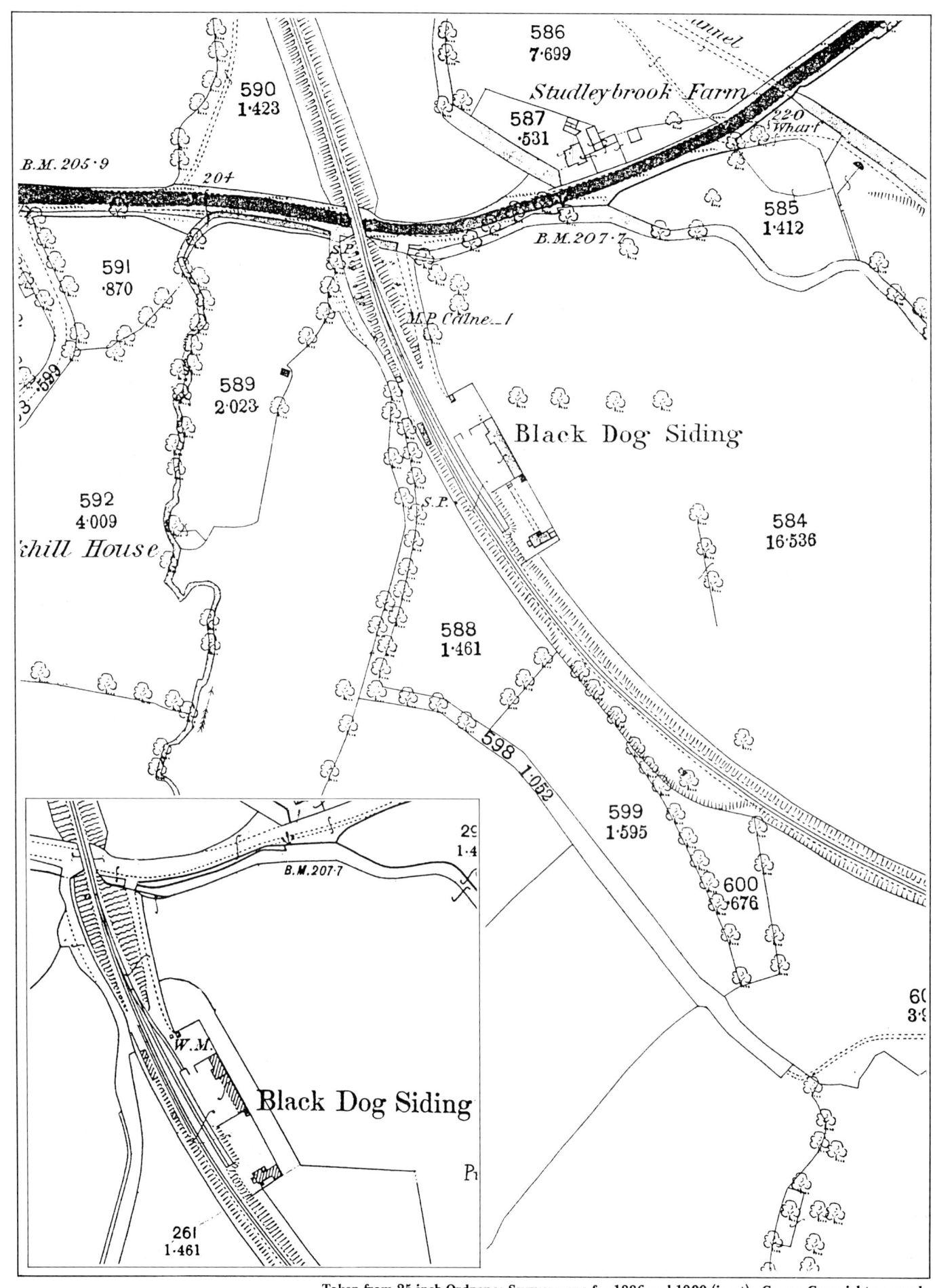

Taken from 25 inch Ordnance Survey maps for 1886 and 1900 (inset). Crown Copyright reserved.

Black Dog Halt on 18th July 1930, just showing the second siding on the left.    Collection D. J. Hyde

notice given at any time to be sufficient to terminate the arrangement.

In 1898 the staff consisted of station master and a foreman, and on 29th March 1921, station master and porter. George Neate, the first station master, was succeeded in June 1911 by William Cockram, previously parcel porter at Chippenham. When he left in 1930 the GWR reconsidered matters. The station master received £4 a week plus an additional 5 per cent from the company to cover his overtime. As annual receipts at Black Dog amounted to only £2,000, R.C. Pole, the Divisional Superintendent at Bristol, believed this insufficient to appoint another station master, preferrring to employ a Grade 1 porter at 48 to 50 shillings. Lord Lansdowne assented and the agreement terminated on 1st July 1930. The post was filled by Douglas Lovelock who had strict instructions not to air any political views. Station master's privileges were withdrawn, the house being let for a nominal rent of £10 per annum, Lord Lansdowne paying rates and repairs but providing no free coal. In 1950 Lovelock purchased the station house. The porter in charge went to Calne on Sundays to assist in loading Harris' parcels, also the extra heavy pre-Christmas traffic there. He also acted as travelling ticket collector on late Sunday evening trains, carrying crowds of returning servicemen to Calne.

Although Lansdowne let other passengers use his station, it did not appear in public timetables. When in April 1898 the GWR requested the Marquess to allow a board bearing the words 'Black Dog Station' on the platform, permission was declined. Not until 15th September 1952 was it a public station, the nameboard being erected just before Christmas 1952. Until that year the halt did not exist for ticket purposes, passengers paying to Calne or Stanley Bridge. On 3rd January 1959, a second class monthly return was bought from Black Dog Halt to Stanley Bridge Halt, the ticket issued being a GWR blank third class card ticket lettered 'Black Dog Siding'. It appears that in GWR days, although passengers were not permitted to book to Black Dog, they were allowed to take return tickets. On 1st February 1960 the station became an unstaffed halt. A second siding added between 1886 and 1900 was removed circa September 1932. When the station became unstaffed, the remaining siding was still available on advance notice being given to the Calne station master. The station closed to goods on 10th June 1963, the siding being lifted 1st November 1963.

In January 1876 Lansdowne was given permission to erect a timber-built waiting shed on the 80ft 6in long platform. costing £59 13s. 2d., it was instated during the winter of 1876–7, having a waiting room at the Calne end and an office at the other. A notice by the telephone advised, 'Don't say "Hello", say "This is Black Dog Sidings speaking"'. William Cockram noticed the office door open one summer's night so he telephoned the police and kept watch until they arrived. They caught the thief cutting open the leather cash bag. In later years it was practice for the porter in charge to send his cash to Calne, where it arrived at 2.6 p.m. and was added to the Calne remittance.

Beyond the ramp at the Calne end was an iron lamp hut. The fairly low standard lamp was replaced by a tall post erected by BR to hold a Tilley lamp, which was hoisted into position when lit. Caring for the environment, the Marquess

**Black Dog Bridge c.1910, looking towards Chippenham.** *Calne Town Council*

was given permission to plant trees on the embankment adjacent to his private station. Although not a block post, Black Dog originally had a signal box and four signals, two either side of the station. The box was erected by the GWR. A quarter of a mile long cinder path linking station and estate was kept in perfect condition by Bowood staff, and received attention at least once a week. To deter the public from crossing the line and exposing themselves to danger, a notice was erected at the foot of the station drive: 'Carriage approach to the station. Foot passengers under the bridge'. In the late 1950s a sign was erected: 'Passengers must not cross the line except by footbridge', but soon dismantled as there was no footbridge. The station was favoured because during the slump of the 1930s, when other stations were neglected, it received a repaint.

Estate traffic consisted of 7–8 trucks of coal two or three times a year, outgoing pit props, silverware regularly loaded and offloaded into vans, and the Marquess's horses being taken to and from stud. The Estate had stables by the loading dock, with standing for about three horses; the building was later used by the coal merchant for stabling his horses. Apart from this traffic to and from Bowood, there was a considerable quantity of other traffic – grain for Moss's Mill, Conygre Mill and Hazeland Mill; W.E. Beint & Sons' timber mill at Derry Hill despatched cut timber as well as boxes sent to South Wales for the transport of tin plate, a man being employed to take these boxes between the works and Black Dog, where they were piled in the yard. Coffin boards also formed outward consignments, but all this ceased in 1960 when it was sent by

**W. H. A. Cockram, station master at Black Dog, with his wife and daughter at the Station House, c.1912.** *A. Cockram*

# ALONG THE ROUTE

This view of Black Dog Halt also features neatly rolled tarpaulins beside the wagons. The parcels office is on the left and the booking office at the far end.
*P. Vines*

'45XX' class 2−6−2T entering Black Dog Halt with a down train c.1938, with wagon sheets in evidence again. *D. Lovelock*

'54XX' class 0–6–0PT No. 6406 arriving at Black Dog with the 4.30 p.m. Chippenham to Calne train. The site of the former carriage loading dock can be seen and also the approach drive and gates to the main road beyond. The thick hedge in the top right-hand corner marked the course of the Wilts & Berks Canal.
*M. E. J. Deane*

A 2-car auto train arriving at Black Dog Halt c.1953, with the former station master's house in the centre of the view and the stables further left.
*M. E. J. Deane*

Black Dog c.1950 before the erection of the nameboard. The sleeper walkway across the tracks gave access to the goods yard.
*M. E. J. Deane*

# ALONG THE ROUTE

'54XX' class 0–6–0PT No. 5423 approaching Black Dog Halt with a down train c.1953.   *T. J. Saunders*

Black Dog ground frame hut in the late 1950s and a close-up of the ground signal and steel sleepers on the main line.   *D. Lovelock*

# 58                    THE CALNE BRANCH

road. In 1962–3 empty coal wagons were placed in the siding for loading with sugar beet, farmers filling a wagon on receipt of a permit from the Ministry of Agriculture.

The short siding was used for loading and unloading road vehicles, including steam rollers, at the carriage dock, and was also used by Beints for bringing small coal to power the saw mill. R.S. Heath had a coal wharf. Coal from Camerton was soft and, if handled too much, it was inclined to break. Instead of taking it out of the wagon, he would leave it in the siding for three or four weeks, happily paying sixpence a day demurrage. The weighbridge was originally installed by the Radstock Coal & Wagon Company which had a wharf at Black Dog. The brick weigh-house with its slate roof was burnt down during World War 2 when the coal merchant drying sacks had too big a fire. Sometimes the sidings at Black Dog were full and wagons consigned there had to be held at Calne until they could be accepted. The sidings were worked by trains in either direction. The procedure for a down train picking up would be that the engine would stop before the ground frame, uncouple and draw forward so the wagon required from the siding could run by gravity on to the train, whereupon the engine would reverse and re-couple. It was also permissible for up to eight wagons to be propelled from Black Dog to Calne. In practice this number was rarely handled at Black Dog, but an occasional wagon was propelled to Calne to avoid stopping on the return journey and thus finish work that much earlier.

A wagon could only be shunted into the siding from an up train.

Snow or ice could cause problems for the first train going up the gradient of 1 in 100 from Black Dog towards Calne. The Calne fixed distant signal stood east of the halt.

## CALNE

Although a terminal station (5 miles 25 chains), the standard GWR red brick buildings of 1895 were parallel to the line to avoid interference with any future extension. The original station, sited slightly nearer the buffer stops, was probably of timber construction. The layout at Calne showed almost continuous growth. As far back as September 1883 the Calne Railway directors pressed the GWR to provide additional accommodation, holding the view that, unless it was speedily supplied, traffic would suffer. The four goods sidings shown on the 1880 Ordnance Survey map grew to five by 1900, seven in July 1906, and eight by the late 1930s. The platform road at the passenger station was extended a few yards east in August 1931 to accommodate one more van. The parcels office was rebuilt at some period and, when the goods shed canopy became redundant, the stanchions were removed to the passenger platform to lengthen the canopy in front of the parcels office and shelter the Harris traffic. To accommodate the eight-coach trains required by the large number of RAF personnel stationed in the vicinity, the platform itself was extended in

Calne fixed distant signal, 1,180 yds from the signal box, c.1960. The portable sign warned of a 20 mph temporary speed restriction ahead.
*M. B. Sadler*

# ALONG THE ROUTE

**An 0–6–0PT pushing two auto cars on a special train between Calne and Black Dog halts during the ASLEF strike on 30th May 1955.**
*D. Lovelock*

1942 as far as the signal box. The cost of this extension was met by the Government, the GWR making repayment after the war. At the same time, a timber-built booking office and waiting room were added near the water tower to cope with the increased number of passengers. Traffic had reached such proportions that parcel and clerical staffs had to be in separate accommodation and during World War 2 it was not unusual for the daily takings to exceed £1,000. Although a sign indicating the location of the new booking office was nailed to the wall on the platform side, it was invisible from the platform entrance, so another was erected at right-angles so that it could be seen from further down the platform. Although another sign projected from the rear of the booking office, most passengers missed seeing it as they tended to approach along the platform rather than along the outside. Also in 1942 a galvanised iron shed was built near the ticket office for the storage of commuters' bicycles, their owners working at such places as Westinghouse and Nestlés, Chippenham. This shed was also used for storing goods safely for collection the following day. RAF camp medical supplies were held there pending collection.

The station was lit by gas but in the 1920s decaying pipes led to a failure one Christmas when candles had to be used.

New piping was laid along the platform facing. This form of lighting needed considerable maintenance, a fitter coming from Swindon every Monday to trim the pilot lights and replace broken mantles. In order to spot a leakage which would have been indicated by a fluctuation in the use of gas, the meter, sited at the town end of Station Road, was read daily by the senior parcels porter on his way to lunch. Not long before the line's closure, electric lighting was installed by Colston Ltd, the Bristol electrical contractors, in May 1961.

### Siding Accommodation from South to North

|  | No. of wagons |  |
|---|---|---|
| Coal siding | 37 | Built late 1930s |
| Mileage siding | 34 | Added July 1906 |
| Mileage siding | 20 | Added July 1906 |
| Loading bank and access to Messrs Harris | 20 |  |
| Loading bank | 17 |  |
| Goods shed road (outside) | 16 |  |
| Goods shed road (inside) | 4 |  |
| Dock road | 20 |  |
| Milk siding or 'Middle road' | 10 |  |
|  | 178 |  |

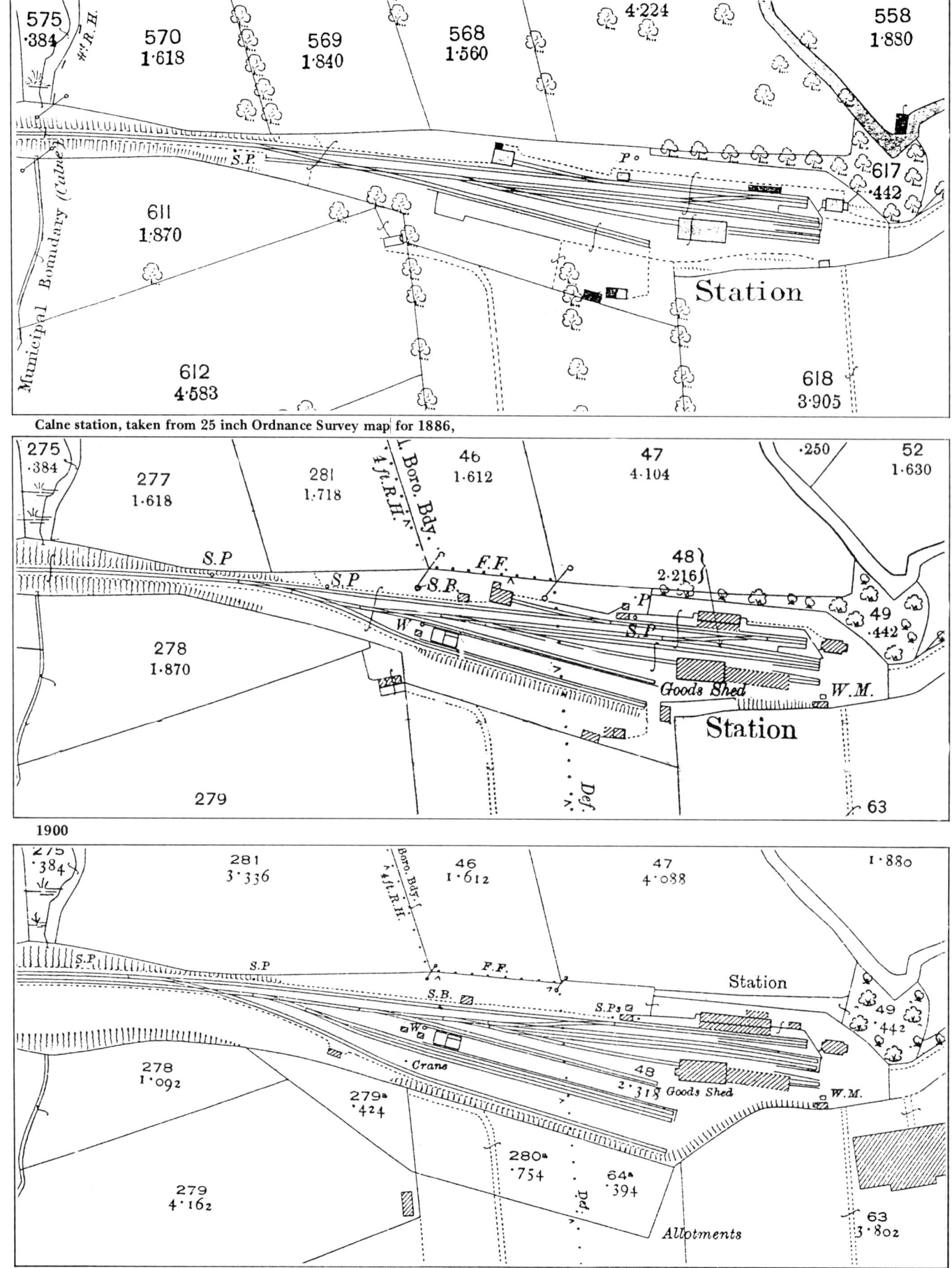

Calne station, taken from 25 inch Ordnance Survey map for 1886,

1900

1923

Crown Copyright reserved.

'850' class 0–6–0ST No. 853 by Calne signal box c.1905, with signalman Arthur Gabb; his son Albert below; George Jones, permanent way packer; fireman Jim Fellander; and an unidentified guard on the right. *Collection P. Vines*

The goods shed, with its stone walls and slated roof, had no doors but was provided with an interior lock-up. Inside was a 30-cwt hand crane and outside a yard crane capable of lifting 5 tons 18 cwt at 60 degrees, the original yard crane being of the small pillar type. The staff room at the west end of the goods shed was colloquially known as the 'bug hole'. The old goods office was demolished and new long galvanised iron goods and weighbridge offices erected at the top of the hill adjacent to Harris' premises. The goods office was heated by two GWR stoves. The 20-ton weighbridge, which, in addition to being used for railway purposes, was also used by the local police for weighing vehicles for taxation, has now been moved to CMA (Calne) Limited, builders' merchants in Oxford Road, Calne. Seven members of staff occupied the goods office in 1947–8, but in mid-1950 when Calne freight was taken over by Chippenham, the staff was reduced to one clerk and a weighbridge lad, and the long hut was replaced c.1951 by a small wooden hut, better suited to the reduced staff.

Circa 1925 the cattle pen sidings had a concrete trough put between the rails to facilitate washing, the siding on the other side of the dock being left on ash ballast. New gate posts for the pens were inserted the wrong way round and when workmen came next day to hang the gates, they had to take the posts out and re-set them.

Incoming traffic to the yard consisted of coal, grain, wagon loads of cattle food from Avonmouth, potatoes, pigs, farm implements, Guinness in three hogsheads and two 'thirty-sixes' for bottling by L.J. Buckeridge. Worthington beer arrived for the Lansdowne Hotel, Liberal Club and Conservative Club, and jam arrived monthly for Wiltshires the grocers. Flour, mostly for the Co-op for bread-making, had to be carried up narrow steps to the chute, railwaymen being paid an extra farthing a sack for this. Flour was also delivered to Pound, Taylor & Collin, Quemerford. Fish arrived for the fish and chip shop, this and other small consignments being delivered by a lad porter on a railway bicycle. Grain arrived for the Calne Milling Company in Mill Street, to store at Blacklands outside Calne, and to Rawlings & Phillips at Upper Quemerford Mill. Very large bags of beet pulp arrived from Bury St Edmunds and Felstead. Taylors, fruiterers of Calne, received fruit by rail, especially plums, a complete van load arriving from Worcester. From about 1958 onwards train loads of fer-

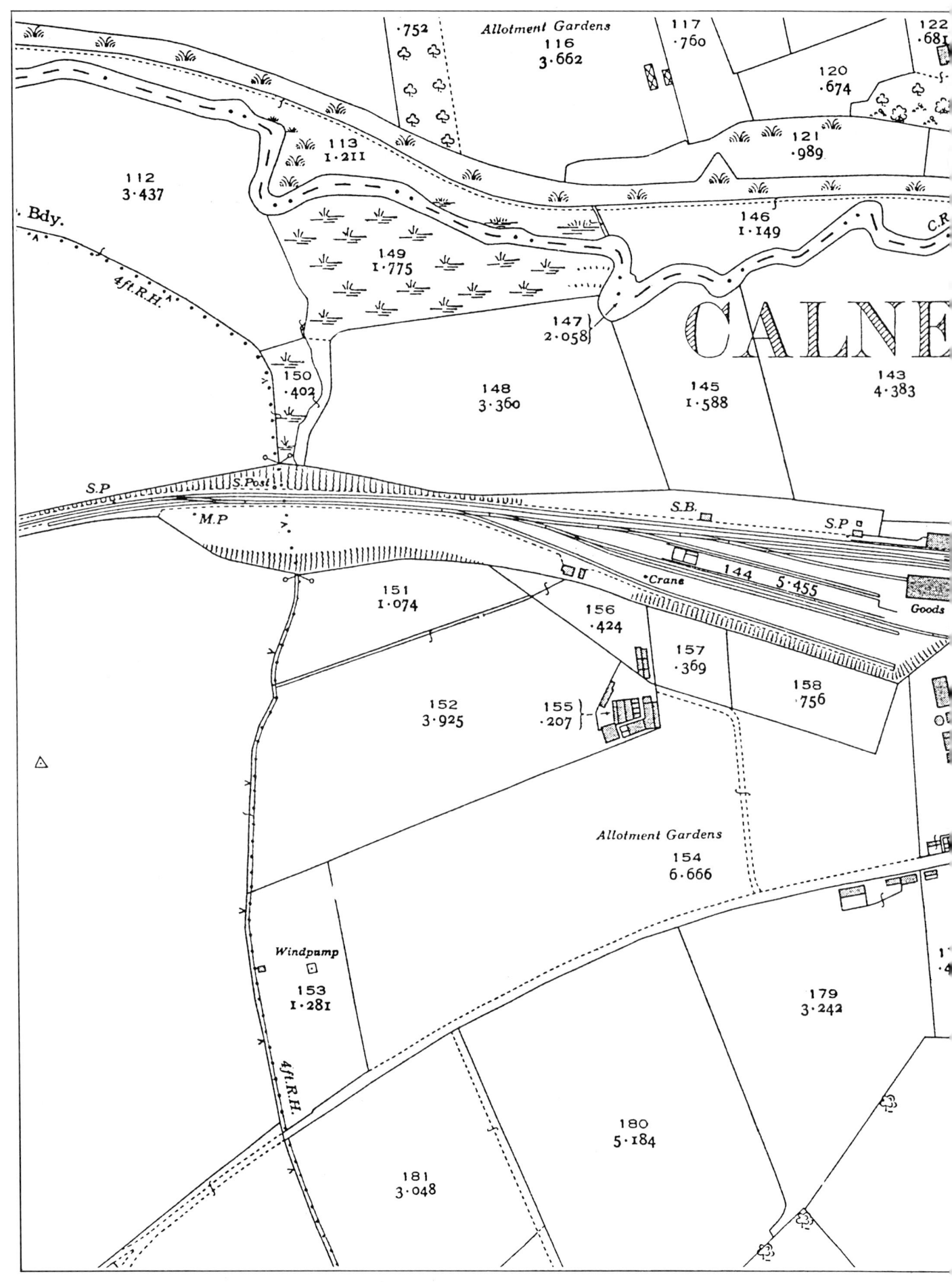

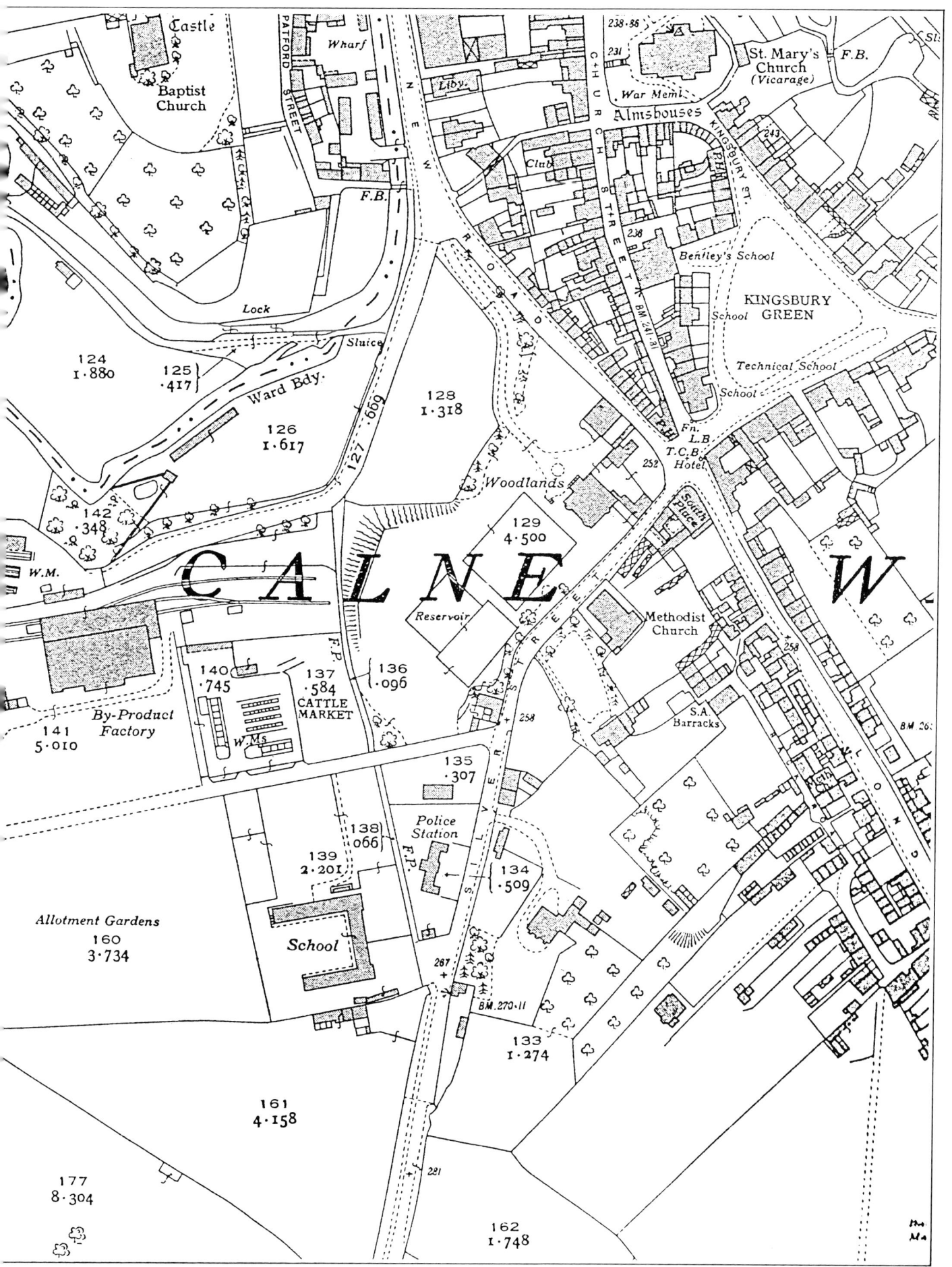

Calne station, taken from 25 inch Ordnance Survey map of 1936. Crown Copyright reserved.

tilisers arrived, about 32 12-ton wagons at a time. A Pannier tank could haul all 32 wagons but a Class 03 0-6-0 diesel could only manage twelve and, as it had to wait for the branch to be clear of passenger trains, it was not always possible to take the whole consignment to Calne in one day. Drapery arrived for drapers, and groceries for the Co-op and Henly's stores. Iron bars came for local blacksmiths.

There were numerous coal merchants: the Co-op, Chivers, F. Angell, H. Symes, A.J. Strange, Fred Stratton, the Calne Coal Company, Thomas Wheeler, and Walter Neate. F.W. Pinniger had a variety of interests and, as well as being a coal merchant, had a dairy and was also a rate collector for the local council. Coal normally arrived in 10-ton wagons, but circa 1947 a 16-ton wagon arrived. Merchants were given the day of arrival and the following day to empty a wagon if they were to avoid demurrage charges. For a one-man concern, and most were, it was easier to unload directly from wagon to lorry, rather than temporarily unload it into the yard. The arrival of this 16-ton wagon threw their economics into chaos as it took longer to unload and more demurrage had to be paid. Gas works coal came from Dodworth and was hauled by Haddrells between station and works. Anthracite and coke arrived for heating the RAF camps, its delivery from the yard being put out to contract. The original coal siding was between the Milk Siding and the Goods Shed Road. When coal wagons were unloaded, inevitably some lumps dropped on the ground. In the case of gas works coal it was not picked up as the thrifty coal merchants would have done, but was rescued by railwaymen anxious to augment their office fires. It was the practice for a tinplate 'blower' to be held in front of the station fires to create a draught and make them burn. They did, and consumed a lot of coal.

Sacks of fat for Messrs Harris arrived from Totnes; this was messy and would seep through the hessian, soiling the boots and trousers of the porters handling it. Imported beef and lamb arrived in insulated containers.

Outward traffic included bacon factory products, RAF stores, sugar beet, and cattle from the market held at Calne on

Calne station c.1900, shortly after rebuilding but before the parcels office extension of the station building or milk platform. The engine shed can be seen between the water tower and signal box. The majority of the track, apart from the crossover, was still flat-bottomed rail at this time.
*Collection D. Lovelock*

Scene at the junction of Station Road with New Road, Calne, c.1895, with the largest timber ever hauled to the station.

*Calne Town Council*

the third Monday of the month, animals being sent to Maiden Lane, London, by a cattle special originating from Warminster and picking up the Calne vans at Chippenham. Circa 1920 three vans of milk left Calne each morning, one in the afternoon, and three in the evening. In the 1950s Mr Henly of Sands Farm sent four or five churns of milk to Paddington daily. During World War 2, trees, cut by landgirls and Italian prisoners-of-war, were brought in by Beint on timber carriages to be despatched by rail and circa 1960 trunks of walnut left destined for France. Also Army tanks were loaded on Warflats at the milk siding, an infrequent traffic, but 15–16 tanks could be loaded without shunting as they could run from truck to truck. One consignment of tanks was taken in two trips because, if made up into one train, the weight was considered excessive for Black Dog Bridge. There was a stud of shire horses at Yatesbury, stallions being walked from the stables to Calne station and loaded into a PACO horse-box with travelling groom.

Simeon Miles, the GWR carter, stabled his horse at the White Hart Hotel. Motor transport was provided for more outlying districts. About 1955 there were two 3-ton Bedford vans, one for the town and another for country parcel delivery. For heavier goods two 5-ton Thornycroft lorries were provided, one delivering round the town and the other to the RAF camps, to Chippenham and half-way to Marlborough, to Goatacre on the Swindon Road and Bromham on the Devizes Road. Later there were 2-ton rigid Austin lorries BR Fleet Nos. 1785 and 2130, plus a 5-ton rigid. No. 1785 was used for town parcel traffic, then went on to Chippenham, returning with local Chippenham–Calne parcels. No. 2130 picked up parcel traffic for delivery in the London Road area and also delivered to the surrounding villages and RAF camps. The 5-tonner delivered full wagon loads.

If the shunter wanted the signalman to set the road for the shunting spur to the platform road he shouted 'Cross the road'. Moving from a siding towards the spur was known as 'Up the Straight'. One shunter had bad feet so consequently rode on the engine step as much as possible. Drivers remember that when he wanted to get off he'd complain, 'Slow down, I can't jump off at this speed. My blasted corns!' Freight facilities were withdrawn from 2nd November 1964, the signal box closed and all track was taken out of use except the platform road.

Traffic at Calne, both passengers and parcels, grew enormously between 1914 and 1920.

| Year | No. of Passengers | Forwarded Parcels & Miscellaneous Traffic | Received Parcels & Miscellaneous Traffic | Tonnage |
|---|---|---|---|---|
| 1914 | 29,211 | 166,469 | 19,411 | 41,391 |
| 1920 | 37,414 | 334,063 | 24,292 | 54,547 |
| Increase | 8,203 | 167,594 | 4,881 | 13,156 |

A busy scene at Calne c.1905. The bank in the foreground was excavated in 1906 to allow one more siding to be laid.
*Author's Collection*

Apart from the Harris traffic and parcels for tradesmen, St Mary's School for Girls, a day and boarding establishment, provided daily and termly traffic, the latter including a considerable quantity of Passengers Luggage in Advance. Towards the end of each term the school forwarded a list of ticket requirements which was fulfilled and the tickets sent to the school. A 5-tonner took a whole morning picking up the trunks. Five to eight vans left Calne on several trains, for various destinations, the last, at 7.5 p.m., taking three to four vans. At the start of a term, luggage arrived piecemeal in the ordinary luggage compartment of the branch train and was stored in the parcel office and galvanised iron shed at the stop block end of the platform for bulk delivery.

In 1898 the staff consisted of a station master, three parcels porters, two porters and two lad porters. By 29th March 1921 this had increased to station master, one chief goods clerk, three goods clerks, two women goods clerks, two parcels clerks, one junior booking clerk, two signalmen, one foreman passenger and goods, one shunter, four parcels porters class 2, one checker, two goods porters, three porters, two lad porters, one charwoman and one supernumerary cattle pen cleaner. Their work was detailed as follows:

'Traffic chiefly consists of small consignments in consequence of which clerical work is heavy and staff employed fully occupied in their duties. The chief goods clerk deals with: district goods manager's correspondence, weekly returns; restrictions and loading arrangements; requisition of error sheets; various returns for the District Goods Manager ledger and station account outstandings, monthly summaries, cash book, credit accounts, advising other clerks on general procedure and regulations, also general supervision of office, shed and yard.

Messrs. Pinniger's wagon No. 2 in black and white livery, built by Gloucester Railway Carriage & Wagon Co., November 1902.
*Author's Collection*

'Clerk 2 Inwards: enter up and check charges, wagon books, ledgers, delivery book, advise warehouse traffic, Inwards credit account.

'Clerk 3 Outwards: outwards correspondence, agents' cartage, adjusting rate cards, route and rate books, Ministry of Transport returns.

'Woman Clerk Outwards: sorting invoices, notes for Harris & Co's rebate, Railway Clearing House Abstracts. Invoicing.

'Woman Clerk 2 Outwards: Ledgers, daily summary of ledger accounts, wagon book, daily loading returns, credit accounts, dispatched letters, attend telephone.

'Booking Clerk: all booking when on duty, prepare passenger accounts and returns.

# ALONG THE ROUTE

'Parcels Clerk 1: Check charges. Prepare Harris' accounts, Deal with parcel correspondence. Keep cash book. In charge of general parcel working.

'Parcels Clerk 2: check charges, keep milk book, prepare traders' accounts, assist with passenger accounts, book one passenger train daily.

'A considerable number of claims for loss, damage, etc are made by Harris & Co. Prior to October 1920 these were dealt with by the station master. Since October, this work has been transferred to the and it is questionable whether the small quantity of milk requires a booked train. If necessary, a special could be run to clear cattle, and the milk could be conveyed by the Sunday evening train from Calne.' [This was not implemented. CGM]

In World War 2 no less than 40 staff were employed at Calne which is indicative of its importance. By 1957–61 the staff on the freight side just consisted of a clerk, yard checker, goods checker, goods porter and three lorry drivers. Wages came by

Postmarked 14th June 1910, this postcard, showing pigs in Station Road, Calne, was addressed to Dr. Wheeler, Medical College, Peking, China. The card travelled via Siberia and was postmarked at Peking 9th July 1910. *Collection P. Q. Treloar*

goods and parcels department, but at present it is in arrears and two relief clerks are bringing all claims up to date.

'Four Class 2 parcel porters, one porter and one lad porter: in addition to parcels office work, these men collect tickets, clean station offices etc and attend to passenger trains. Fully employed.

'In addition to the Great Western men in the yard, considerable assistance is given by Harris who employ three men to assist with handling traffic on the GW goods platform.

'One lad porter attends cart weighbridge, obtaining mileage signature, enters up wagon books and advises mileage traffic. A supernumerary is employed cleaning cattle pens and trucks at the approximate cost of £31 p.a. The porter at Black Dog Siding does not appear to be fully employed, his appointment being necessary in connection with the 8 hour day. Supernumerary duties at Calne could be performed by him in addition to his work at Black Dog Siding. Supernumerary works for about two hours daily.

'On Sunday an engine and van leaves Chippenham at 6.40 a.m. for Calne, returning at 7.45 a.m. with the milk traffic. 26 churns each Sunday, which is light. In addition to milk traffic, this train conveys any cattle traffic which accumulates at Chippenham over Saturday night. Service requires foreman, signalman and shunter travelling safe, arriving at 12.12 pm on Thursdays. They were made up by the booking clerk and paid out by the station master, clerks later carrying out this duty. Staff at Chippenham were paid 'Industrial' rates and worked a 44-hour week, whereas Calne was classified 'Rural' where a 48-hour week was worked for less pay. Allotments were provided alongside the line for staff to grow vegetables.

Staff were imaginative and innovative and in the summer of 1959 when there was no threat of closure, long before the general distribution of pocket timetables, the booking office staff duplicated pocket timetables giving times of branch trains.

## Booking Clerk's Day

On arrival at 6.15 a.m. the booking clerk took the key to the ticket case out of the date press where it was hidden, opened the case and removed the key to the outer safe door. Each of the three booking clerks held a personal key for the inner safe door which was then opened. He then started booking

Calne in 1925. The space between the signal box and water tower was originally occupied by the engine shed. Remnants of the original flat-bottomed rails still serve the cattle dock on the right.

*C. L. Mowat*

passengers for the first train, the 6.35 a.m. Monday mornings were more hectic than others as weekly seasons needed to be issued. Ninety-nine per cent of the workmen who travelled on the branch were employed by Westinghouse. Children attending education authority schools had season tickets overprinted 'Wilts EA' in red, to prevent anyone trying to obtain a refund. The early turn booking clerk was on until 1.15 p.m., six days a week, the late turn clerk working from 2–9 p.m. The parcels porter was supposed to book passengers when the booking office closed, but apparently he didn't – instead they were excessed at Chippenham. At weekends the booking office staff rattled out tickets to Bath and Bristol like shelling peas from a pod, £200 or more being taken on a Saturday. That day Forces' leave returns to Chippenham and Bath were not put in the dispenser; clerks just split the 250 out and issued from the pile, thus saving valuable seconds. The booking office held Calne 'A' Stock (secondary stock) so that at busy times, two booking clerks could operate, the assistant being seconded from the parcels office. During such rush hours a parcels clerk sat between and behind the two booking clerks and kept the blank card register.

A split turn was worked on Sunday from 10.45 a.m.–12.15 p.m. and 5.0 p.m.–10.45 p.m. Sundays were relatively quiet and allowed time for the 'weekly proof'. This was checking cash and credit balance with tickets issued, then working out the revenue return for the week.

On 18th December 1958 explosives were used to blow open the booking office safe, the blast damaging the office itself. The robbery was on a Thursday night, carefully chosen as normally there would have been a large cash content following a ticket sales visit to the RAF camps. However, that particular night there was less money than usual as many servicemen were absent on block leave. Following this incident less cash was held at Calne, the majority being placed in a travelling safe and sent to Chippenham where it spent the night in the safe there, returning to Calne on the 6.15 a.m. next morning. It was safer at Chippenham because the station was continuously manned. Cash at Calne was made up at 5 p.m. each day and sent to the district office at Westbury on the 7.25 a.m. ex Calne, other stations en route dropping cash into the safe which returned on the train arriving at 12.12 p.m. back at Calne. Cash taken after 5 p.m. was put with the next day's takings. The porter at Black Dog sent his cash in the official bag to Calne on the train which arrived at 2.6 p.m.

The trade of Messrs Harris' bacon factory was always important to the Calne branch. In September 1876 Harris complained about the lack of illumination which caused great inconvenience when unloading pigs at night whilst in October 1890 complaints were received regarding insufficient accommodation for unloading pigs. Before World War 1 Harris' outwards traffic travelled in ordinary passenger brake vans, the special branded vehicles not being used until the post-war

**Branded vans being loaded at Calne in the late 1920s. The nearest worked Calne–Southampton and the second Calne–Paddington. The nearest platform barrow contains boxes of lard and sausages.**
*E. Gross*

The perishable traffic at this time was carried mostly in Siphon C vehicles, pictured above.
*E. Gross*

One of Harris's vans in the station yard at Calne. The notice on the side of the cart reads 'Bacon curers to HM King George VI'.
*Calne Town Council*

period. It was roughly about this time that Harris built a new, larger factory, two imposing dwellings being demolished for its site. Construction materials came by rail, bricks from Cattybrook, girders from South Lambeth and cement from Penarth. Harris' hangar, sited just east of the railway yard, dealt with pigs' hair for brushes, bone meal, dried blood and offal for fertiliser, and incoming traffic such as soya flour, salt in Salt Union wagons, tins, cartons and coal. The building came from the World War 1 Royal Flying Corps station at Yatesbury. The fact that it had once been an aircraft hangar may have been why the nearby market was bombed in 1941. The hangar preceded the by-products factory and private sidings provided under an agreement, signed on 26th March 1928, the Great Western being responsible for their maintenance. Two sidings served the firm's warehouse, whilst beyond were two tracks for stabling wagons conveying coal for the factory's boilers, 10–12 wagons of small coal arriving each week. The factory changed to gas fuel before the closure of the Calne branch and the siding agreement was terminated late in 1964. The gate across Harris' sidings was never closed. The sidings were shunted twice daily, 7.30–8.0 a.m. and a bigger shunt in the afternoon. A wagon load of bacon was sent out to Bristol on Mondays, Wednesdays and Fridays, and to Paddington on Tuesdays and Thursdays. This bacon traffic left direct from the hangar rather than the passenger platform where smaller parcels were dealt with. 1½ cwts of bacon wrapped in hessian were moved up from the factory to the siding by horse and cart and was offloaded into vans at the hangar. Harris's had a special rate from Calne to Paddington, so although goods might be labelled to an ultimate address in the eastern counties, for instance, they were placed in the Paddington van and marked 'London Re-Book' so that Harris's could take advantage of its special rate to London for part of the journey. Messrs Harris's goods revenue account totalled £1,000 each month, whilst on the passenger side, Calne outwards parcel revenue was, in the Bristol division, second only to Temple Meads.

On each shift Harris's men came up from the factory with a horse and cart loaded with parcels, unhitched the horse and took back an empty cart which had already been unloaded. The carter started work at 8.30 a.m. Mondays to Wednesdays and went on till 7 p.m., taking only an hour's break for lunch. He made up to 44 trips each day. The horse was replaced about 1950 by a Scammell mechanical horse which left a trailer at the station to be unloaded while it took back an empty. The parcels were loaded into Siphons, several branch trains hauling one or more branded vans. The train which left Calne at 2.20 p.m. carried the Paddington van; the 5.0 p.m. took the Manchester and Cardiff van, the latter in later years running on to Pembroke. The 5.35 p.m. Calne to Westbury conveyed the Portsmouth van. The Paddington, Newcastle on Tyne, and Bristol vans travelled with the 7.5 p.m. ex Calne, the engine having to run round because a B-set was used for the service. The vans returned in due course, that to Newcastle taking two days to get back. Sometimes they went missing and a hue and cry had to be raised to get them back because they were so convenient to load. These branded vans had transfers in them for many places – for example the Portsmouth van had transfers for Westbury, Warminster, Salisbury, Southampton and Eastleigh; and the Newcastle van for Swindon, Oxford, Banbury, Leicester, Nottingham and York. Local traffic to Box etc, travelled in the luggage compartment of ordinary trains.

Despatch was very efficient, sausages made after 7.30 a.m. being delivered to Bath shops soon after 10 a.m.

The 11.5 a.m. Sunday train ex Calne conveyed no less than five vans (Siphon Gs as opposed to the branded Siphon Cs) with three pairs of doors for easy loading. Three of these vans were for the parcels train to Swindon and destined for Paddington, Manchester and Newcastle on Tyne, one to Portsmouth and another for Cardiff. These Sunday vans carried tons of black puddings. Sunday traffic was all 'ledger labelled' – a ledger label being an account holder. Two railwaymen went to Harris's factory on Friday to ledger label the goods which were then taken to the station on Sunday morning and loaded between 7 and 11 a.m.

The first system for Harris' parcels was sticking on railway stamps valued according to weight and distance. The second system used was ledger labels bearing a serial number, but no price, the parcel clerks (plus a parcel porter on one day a week) recording the price on an abstract – foolscap paper which was submitted for payment. This earned the railway up to £4,000 per month. The third and final system was the Ledger account prepared at the factory instead of the station. This meant that parcels could be loaded straight into the vans. Two parcel porters attended to the stamps and ledger at the factory. Ledg-

**Arthur Burchell, the Harris's carter, with his horse, Violet in Station Road c.1930. They transported goods between the factory and the station.** *P. Vines*

A. I. Hillier's son in their Morris Commercial, with a load of churns at the approach to the milk dock. *P. Vines*

ering of the Sunday traffic was carried out in Harris's chill room on Saturday.

After about 1951, a pig special ran every Sunday morning, pigs coming from Camborne, Bodmin and Taunton where Saturday markets were held. Some pigs came from the Queen's herd at Sandringham. One Sunday there were 100 pig trucks which had to be taken over in several trains. On this occasion pigs were kept in the station yard at Calne for two days, the Harris' factory having insufficient lairage. Cattle trucks bringing the pigs had to be cleaned, whitewashed and returned. A truck load of pigs' hair crawling with maggots was sent away each Saturday morning in an open wagon. Because of the horrible stench, the driver did not want it near his engine, nor the guard by his van. On one occasion, for a joke, the

A. I. Hillier's 30 cwt Morris Commercial lorries. Hillier collected churns from farms in the Heddington, Blackland and Calstone areas and delivered them to Calne station. *P. Vines*

J. H. Blackford & Sons' gang at work on laying Harris's water main at Calne c.1932. The cleaner areas on the end of the goods shed show where the canopy was.
*Calne Town Council*

Chippenham shunters put the wagon by the down platform. Its offensive smell soon made its presence felt and the station master phoned through to the goods yard and asked them to remove it. Normally it was placed on the up side awaiting transfer in the afternoon to Marsh & Baxter, at Brierley Hill, another part of the Harris combine.

Water was of prime importance both as a cleansing agent and a raw material. With the expansion of the factory, water supply proved a problem, the amount purchased from the Calstone Water Company being restricted. A test bore made on Harris's own property proved completely dry. About 1932 the Pearce Brewery at Langley Burrell was placed on the market, comprising a house, two cottages, the brewery and an existing borehole so Messrs Harris purchased the whole property as a promising site for further drilling. Following a trial 18in diameter bore reaching a depth of 345ft, a 6ft diameter well was dug by men normally employed in the Staffordshire coalfield. The two gangs of six men each were glad to be offered this job during the trade depression. The well provided a good continuous supply of 10,000 galls per hour. Two Sulzer 9-stage pumps were used to raise it from a standing water level of 80ft. A 9in diameter bitumen lined steel pipe was laid across pastures, passing under the GWR Chippenham to Swindon main line to reach the Calne branch at a point about 100 yds the Chippenham side of Black Bridge, the pipeline then following the railway to Calne station. A water treatment plant was built adjacent to Messrs Harris' private siding. Treated water was stored in a 500,000 gallon reservoir, but after about two years it became apparent that the water was very corrosive, leaks appearing in tanks and pipework at an alarming rate, whilst at the well itself, the cast iron pumps suffered from black ferrous oxide. Repairs to the 9in main were frequently required and if a ganger walking the length observed a leak, he notified Messrs Harris. As repair work had to be carried out adjacent to the running line, in the interests of safety a look-out was necessary, for which the GWR charged something like £1 a day. The North Wilts Water Board considered purchasing the Langley well but did not proceed, whilst about the same time, BR decided to demolish Black Bridge which would have necessitated re-routeing the water main. In 1969 Harris ceased to be supplied with Langley water.

There was a good relationship between firm and railway, Harris's generously giving Calne and Chippenham station and permanent way staff a large pork pie and 1lb of sausages each Christmas.

# GREAT WESTERN RAILWAY

Calne Station Staff.
1911

Calne staff in the 1930s. Back row, left to right: shunter B. Lee; porter Barker; parcels porter E. Granger; parcels porter F. Brittain; porter Wilson; parcels porter A. Lees. Front row: parcels porter E. Ponting; clerk; booking clerk; station master S. Harding; parcels clerk P. Gleed (later station master); leading parcels porter S. King; station foreman H. Poole.  *P. Vines*

# THE STAFF — GREAT WESTERN RAILWAY

Inside the parcels office c.1930. Left to right: parcels porter Ewart Ponting; chief parcels clerk B. J. Shepherd; parcels porter Harry Hitchens; parcels porter Frank Brittain; relief man Fred Clarke; porter Percy Vines. Parcels stamps are in the case to the right. *P. Vines*

Lad porter Ron Truckle, Leslie Kirton (Harris's employee, recording parcels despatched from Calne), and lad porter Jim Wiltshire, seen at Calne during the 1930s. *P. Vines*

Goods guard Charlie Parsons, a 1930s portrait. *P. Vines*

# THE CALNE BRANCH

'45XX' 2–6–2T No. 5511 arriving at Calne with one of Harris's branded Siphons as tail traffic on the 12.28 p.m. ex Bristol Temple Meads in 1939. Moss's Corn Mill is featured in the right background, with the Wilts & Berks Canal running between the two sets of buildings.
*E. J. M. Hayward*

Calne station was used by traffic for RAF Compton Bassett, responsible for training ground wireless operators, and Yatesbury for the training of wireless operators/air gunners, the latter in September 1940 reclassified as signallers, which reflected their task more accurately. In the post-war period Yatesbury was responsible for the more highly skilled wireless trades and Compton Bassett for the less skilled, that is, teleprinter operators and telephone operators.

Yatesbury airfield opened in 1916, closed in 1919, and re-opened in 1935. No. 2 Electrical & Wireless School was formed on 13th October 1938 for training in a large hutted camp alongside the airfield. The sectional wooden buildings for Yatesbury were brought to Calne by rail and provided accommodation for 10,000. When completed, similar construction work began on No. 3 RAF Radio School at Compton Bassett. The branch line then had to deal with a total of 20,000 personnel and their supplies. No. 3 Radio School, Compton Bassett, closed 3rd November 1964 and Yatesbury in April 1969.

Traffic for RAF Lyneham came to Calne to a certain extent because, although Dauntsey was the nearest railway station, it was unable to handle bulky consignments such as aero engines and other large aircraft parts. Coal and coke arrived for the three camps, and there was lots of baggage, especially when married quarters started at Lyneham, when carpets would arrive. Although the railway delivered daily to married quarters and NAAFIs (several at each of the three camps), anything addressed to the Commanding Officer was collected by RAF transport. Railway containers of types A, B, BD and BK were used for the camps, an RAF lorry taking them to Lyneham. However, because Yatesbury and Compton Bassett only had covered vans, they were unable to transport them and so transhipped the goods at Calne. Air Movements Section baggage arrived at Lyneham by air from overseas and was despatched by rail from Calne to various destinations. Lyneham sent off aero engines weekly in 10–15 wagons, the yard crane being used to transfer engines complete with metal stands to SHOCKFIT wagons. The engines were firmly chocked in the trucks with wooden scotches, then roped and sheeted. Other aero engines went away in wooden crates. The small crane in the goods shed was used for lifting the smaller engines. Other items were despatched to maintenance units at Carlisle, Hartlebury, Heywood and Stafford, Calne displaying sagacity by keeping outwards goods to make up full wagon loads so that Calne was credited with traffic instead of Chippenham. RAF motor transport in the form of jeeps, buses and aircraft-towing tractors arrived and were despatched by rail. When loaded, a vehicle had to be tested under the gauge and, if it failed to pass, its tyres were deflated. Crash-damaged aircraft were a common sight in Calne yard and after World War 2 a whole train of Spitfires from Lyneham was despatched for disposal, the wagons carrying them being linked by two parallel instanter couplings. During the war quite a number of coffins containing RAF personnel were carried. A VANFIT was swept out and the coffin ceremonially placed inside by RAF colleagues.

Flight Lieutenant Selby, Railway Transport Officer based at Chippenham station, organised service specials, assisted by a sergeant and a couple of corporals. If it was necessary for service personnel trains to depart soon after one another, one would be loaded at either the cattle bank, or the Middle Road. A major exodus took place prior to a Bank Holiday two or three specials running from Calne. A pair of 2–6–2Ts, or 57XX Panniers, coupled on the empty coaching stock train at Chippenham and took 10–14 coaches to Calne. If proceeding in the up direction on arrival back at Chippenham, points were clipped at the east end of the layout and the main line engine took the train onwards. If going in the other direction, the Panniers would be cut off at the down platform and a larger engine would be attached. The RAF sent postings lists on Mondays so that tickets could be made up in advance for movements from the camps, which normally took place on a Wednesday when trainees left and were replaced by a new batch.

The Air Ministry endeavoured to route personnel by rail as much as possible, so much so that on one occasion a party from Compton Bassett to Lyneham travelled by coach from Compton Bassett to Calne, by rail from Calne to Dauntsey, and by coach from Dauntsey to Lyneham. This involved a rail journey of 11¾ miles plus 7 miles by road, against a direct road distance of 4 miles! A journey from Compton Bassett to Upavon similarly used coach to Calne, rail through Holt Junction and

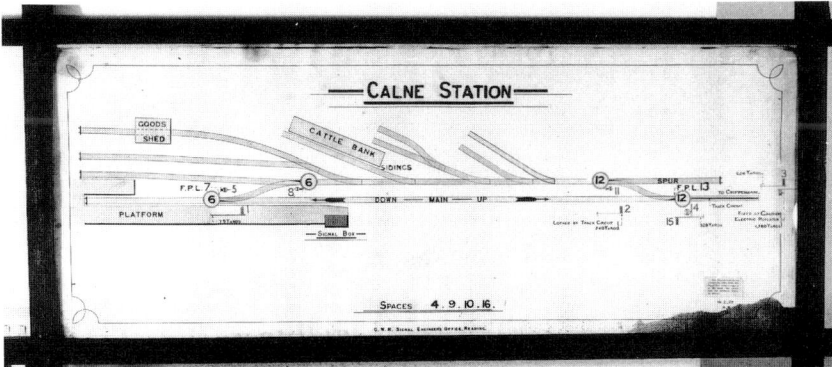

Diagram from Calne signal box. The mark in the bottom right-hand corner was caused by grease when the frying pan was used in the signal box.
*D. Lovelock*

Calne signal box before the platform extension engulfed the well-kept garden surrounding the box.  *Author's Collection*

Calne goods yard c.1962.

D. Lovelock

**Calne, from the cattle pens.** This view, taken c.1951, shows the 1942 extension to the passenger platform, with 2–6–2T No. 5566 heading the 1.12 p.m. (Saturdays only) to Weston-super-Mare.

*M. E. J. Deane*

Devizes to Pewsey, and bus from Pewsey to Upavon – 27½ miles by rail plus 7 miles by road, compared with a direct road mileage of 16. Sometimes the GWR took one or two men unofficially from Calne to Lyneham by lorry, if there was one going there, so they would avoid the rail detour. In 1963 Calne dealt with 6,132 RAF travel warrants.

On Thursday evenings, using a special pass, a member of the Calne booking office staff travelled to Compton Bassett, and another to Yatesbury, on a railway lorry, to sell tickets at the camps in an attempt to avoid long weekend queues at the station. Each booking clerk had a small case labelled Camp A or Camp B containing tickets for main destinations and blanks. One series of tickets was printed for Camp A and another for Camp B. The total collected from the two camps could sometimes amount to over £1,000 which it is said was left overnight at Calne police station for safekeeping.

**Calne, c.1950.**

*J. H. Moss*

A Collett 0—4—2T arriving at Calne, where a heavy load of mail awaits loading.

W. A. Camwell

# ALONG THE ROUTE

Ticket office and waiting room, left.  *D. J. Hyde*

View towards Chippenham in August 1964.
*D. J. Hyde*

Calne station staff 1946. In the back row from left to right are clerk Keith Hillier; weighbridge lad John Wilkins; chief parcels clerk Mr. Williams; unknown; R. Britton; booking clerk Mrs. K. Williamson; booking clerk Mr. Clark. Front row: parcels porter Ewart Ponting; parcels clerk Molly Burchell; lad porter Frank Fields; lad porter Monty Fell. *Collection J. Clapp*

'45XX' class 2–6–2T running round its train, the 1.12 p.m. Saturdays only, c.1950. The crowd of passengers (mainly male) waiting for the train include RAF personnel.
*M. E. J. Deane*

*J. H. Moss*

## ALONG THE ROUTE

Looking towards the buffer stops in June 1964, with a van for Harris traffic in the platform road.  *D. J. Hyde*

The station forecourt. *K. Williams*

Calne from the blocks c.1962, showing the large sign which directed passengers round the outside of the station to the booking office. The RAF Yatesbury notice gave information regarding travel arrangements to the camp whilst the BR poster offered day excursion fare to Newport and Cardiff and specially reduced weekend tickets from Calne to various destinations. *Lens of Sutton*

Entrance to the goods yard (left) and passenger station (right). *K. Williams*

Looking past the weighbridge and office to the goods yard in 1964. *D. J. Hyde*

The west side of the goods shed from the end of the cattle bank, August 1964. *D. J. Hyde*

# ALONG THE ROUTE

This view of the yard shows the cattle bank and the siding to Harris's factory crossing the road. On the left the complete stock of a farm was being moved from Calstone, near Calne, to Cornwall. *D. Lovelock*

Another view of the yard c.1962. The grab in the right foreground was used for unloading wagons of feedstuffs. *D. Lovelock*

One porter has vivid memories of survivors from the Dunkirk evacuation arriving at Calne in 1940. He should have finished work at 10 p.m., but was busy until 6 a.m. next morning dealing with the arrival of several special trains of survivors – some without clothes and some suffering badly from shell shock. One member of staff remembers that the triangular bandages worn by the returning wounded were yellow instead of the usual white. Weapons brought back from Dunkirk were locked up safely in the ladies' waiting room.

During World War 2 staff took paid turns at nightly fire watching in case enemy aircraft dropped incendiary bombs. They slept on old camp beds in the goods office which was heated by a tortoise stove. On one occasion the metal chimney leading smoke out through the timber roof glowed red hot and there were moments of panic until the fire had been damped down sufficiently to avoid danger. On 16th September 1941 three bombs dropped on the market, one man being killed. Lumps of concrete were scattered, damaging vans placed against the blocks at the platform. As a souvenir, one piece of this concrete was inscribed with the date and incorporated into the bottom step of the signal box. There were two passengers on the platform when the raid began, and staff remember the lady saying, 'We must take shelter, uncle, we must take shelter.' So they went through a fence and sheltered under a bramble bush. Shunter Bert Lee and Guard Bill Read more wisely took refuge under a railway van.

Gun and shell cases arrived by rail for Simons Garage in Oxford Road, where further work was carried out on them before being returned. During the war one station master cut pencils in half and inserted them into a metal holder for economy. After the war the brick air raid shelter was converted into the passenger foreman's office.

'57XX' class 0-6-0PT No. 3739 at Calne c.1962. The yard crane had a lifting capacity of 5 ton 18 cwt.  *D. Lovelock*

Another view of the yard c.1962 with the coal siding in the foreground.  *D. Lovelock*

A Spitfire fighter aircraft after loading in the 1940s,  *D. Lovelock*

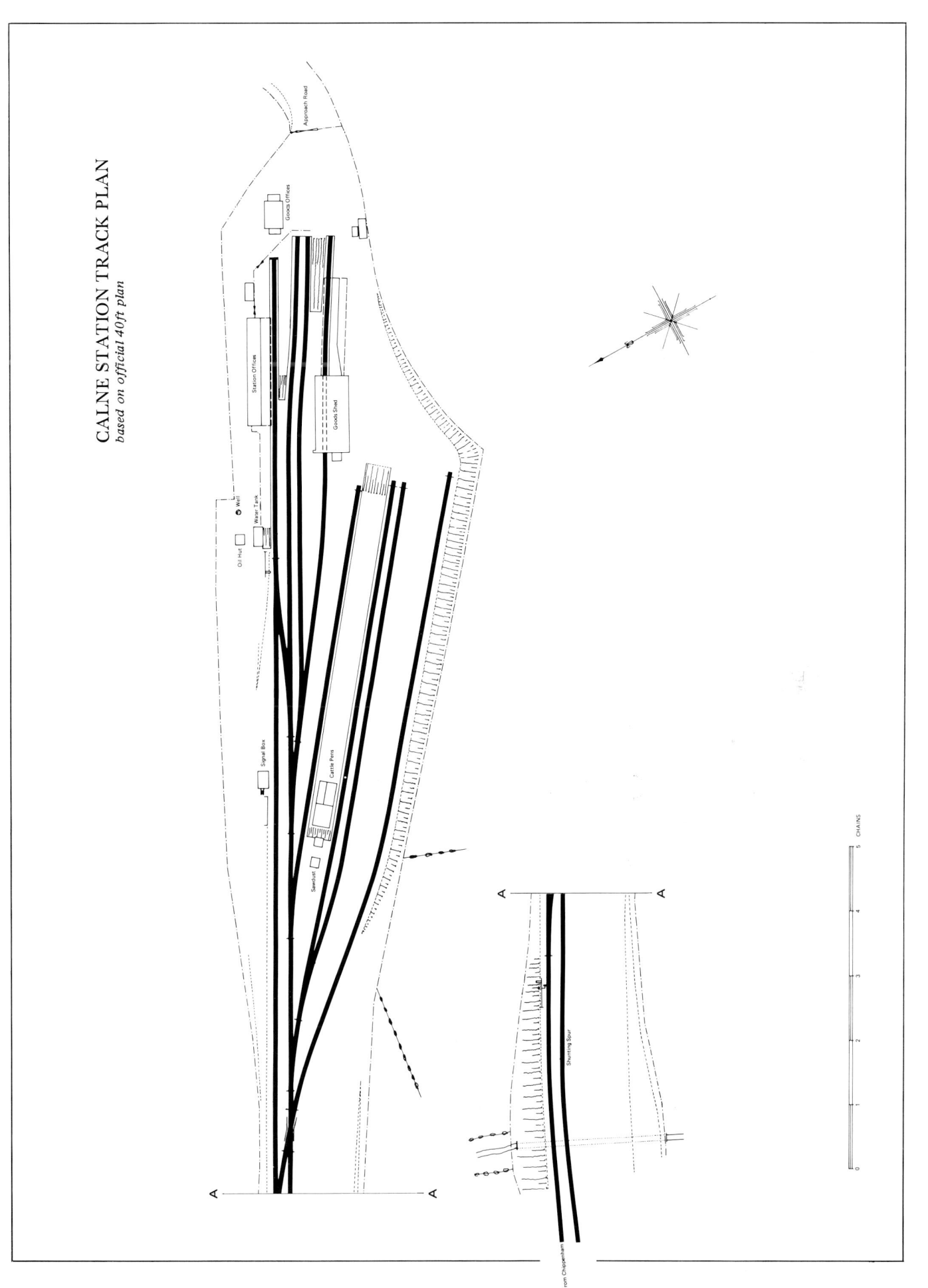

A train leaving Calne for Chippenham. *J. H. Moss*

Various small buildings at the Chippenham end of the station. *K. Williams*

# CHAPTER FIVE
# LOCOMOTIVES AND ROLLING STOCK

Chippenham shed on 17th April 1938, with *Left road:* '45XX' class 2–6–2T No. 5559; '8750' class 0–6–0PT No. 3764; *Centre:* '74XX' class 0–6–0PT No. 7418; '655' class 0–6–0PT No. 2720; Collett 0–4–2T No. 4833; *Right road:* '655' class 0–6–0PT No. 1789. The coal stage on the right was rarely used.
*R. J. Buckley*

THE branch was worked principally by tank engines, usually 0-4-2Ts on passenger and 0-6-0Ts on goods trains. In 1903, apart from the Calne branch engine, some trains were worked by the Chippenham shunting engine and some by the Dauntsey bank engine. Around this time '517' class 0-4-2T No. 853 was recorded as working on the branch. In 1932, No. 4800, the first Collett 0-4-2T, arrived ex works, and locomotives of this class replaced those of the '517' variety, Nos 4833 and 4836 being two further examples which appeared. The 48XX class was later renumbered as the 14XX series. Through trains from Westbury were usually worked by a 54XX class 0-6-0PT. Although officially forbidden, an ex works 94XX class 0-6-0PT worked over the branch on the Saturday through train for Weston-super-Mare. Some through trains were headed by 45XX or 55XX 2-6-2Ts, these classes also appearing on some freight trains. Latterly, ballast trains were usually worked by a '2251' class 0-6-0 tender engine, as there was a likelihood that a tank engine would have run out of water whilst on this duty which involved much waiting about. 0-6-0s of the Dean Goods or '2251' classes sometimes appeared on goods workings, proceeding tender first to Calne to make shunting easier. Named engines were very rare, the first probably being 4-4-0 No. 3829 *County of Merioneth* in the 1926 General Strike, while in the early 1940s 4-4-0 No. 3443 *Chaffinch* hauled an RAF personnel train from Calne to Chippenham on the first leg of its trip to Paddington.

The Calne branch was unusual for a short terminal line in that it was worked by locomotives from no less than four depots – Bath, Westbury, Chippenham and Bristol.

The route colour for the branch was yellow, but yellow-coded engines were not permitted to work into Black Dog bank siding. Speed on the branch was restricted to 30 m.p.h., with a 15 m.p.h. restriction from the quarter-mile post to the main line and vice versa. The 30 m.p.h. limit was not always heeded, Kenneth Leech having timed trains at 50 m.p.h. The fastest recorded journey over the branch is held by Ernie Burrows of the small Bath shed, who with a 45XX 2-6-2T pre-1939, reached Chippenham East signal box with the 10.50 a.m. from Calne in 7½ minutes, making an average speed of about 43 m.p.h. Bert Taylor of Westbury shed took a 54XX class 0-6-0PT with the 12.54 p.m. passenger Chippenham to Calne in 8 minutes.

Ex LMS Ivatt Class 2 2-6-0s and 2-6-2Ts worked on the branch while BR Standard Class 3 2-6-2T No. 82009 first appeared on Saturday afternoon, 23rd June 1955. No. 82001 of the same class hauled the 1.7 p.m. Calne to Weston-super-Mare on 15th August 1964, the last booked steam-hauled train over the branch.

89

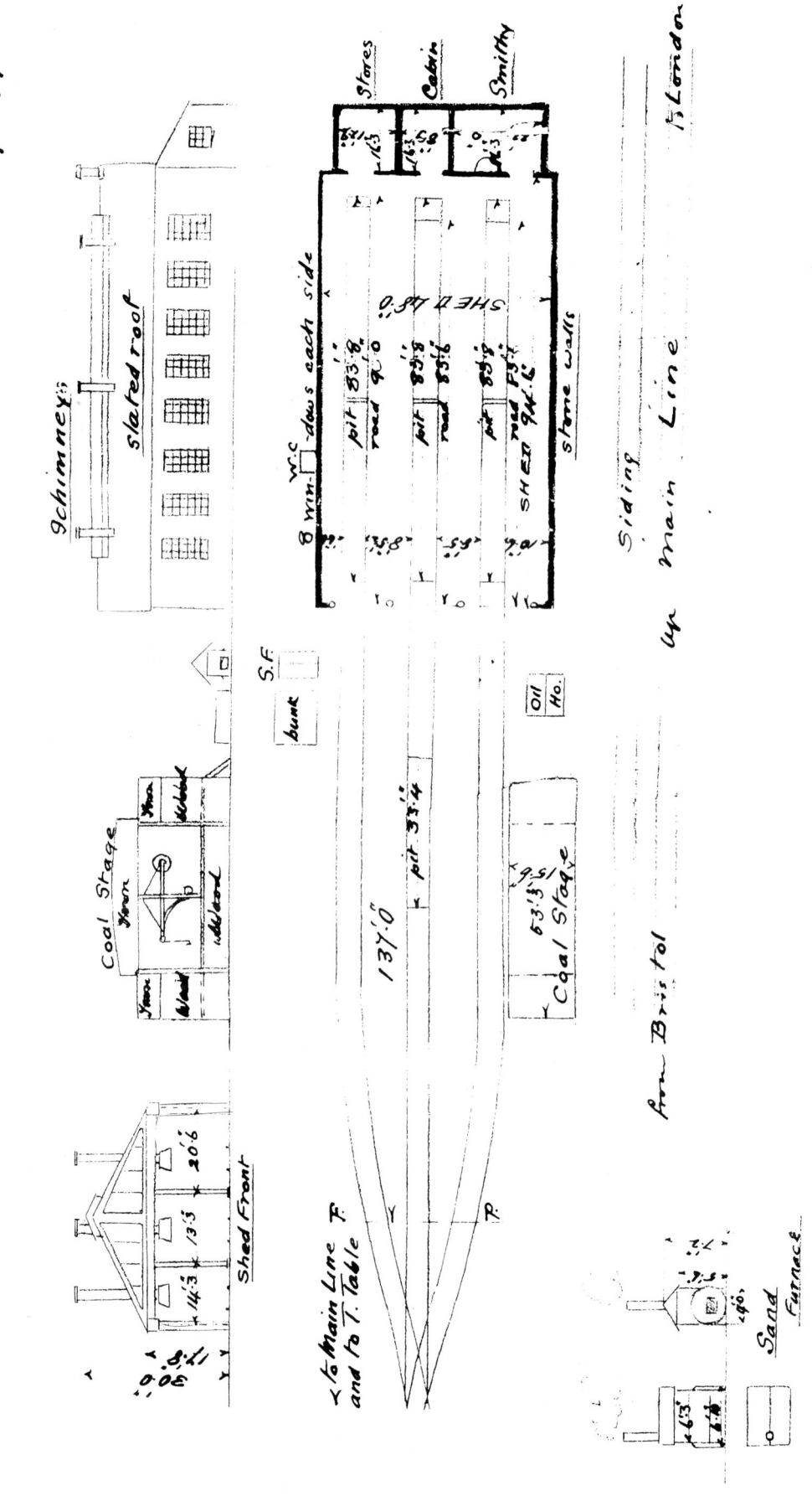

Chippenham engine shed, taken from the official survey, 29th January 1897.

# LOCOMOTIVES AND ROLLING STOCK

**Engine Loads for Passenger, Parcels, Milk & Fish:**
Chippenham–Calne 274 tons
Calne–Chippenham 252 tons
for BR Standard Class 3 2-6-2T, and 2-6-2Ts Nos 4401–10, 4500-99, 5500-74, 0-6-0PTs 36XX, 37XX, 46XX, 57XX, 77XX, 87XX, 96XX, 97XX, 84XX, 94XX.
Restriction of 242 tons to Calne and 220 tons to Chippenham for 0-6-0 and 0-6-0Ts in A Group.
Maximum Loads Chippenham–Calne 35 wagons; Calne–Chippenham 40 wagons.

| Group | Class of traffic | No. of wagons | Direction |
|---|---|---|---|
| A | 1 | 21 | Down |
| A | 1 | 14 | Up |
| A | 2 | 25 | Down |
| A | 2 | 17 | Up |
| A | 3 | 32 | Down |
| A | 3 | 21 | Up |
| A | Empties | 42 | Down |
| A | Empties | 28 | Up |
| B | 1 | 24 | Down |
| B | 1 | 16 | Up |
| B | 2 | 29 | Down |
| B | 2 | 19 | Up |
| B | 3 | 36 | Down |
| B | 3 | 24 | Up |
| B | Empties | 48 | Down |
| B | Empties | 32 | Up |
| C | 1 | 26 | Down |
| C | 1 | 17 | Up |
| C | 2 | 31 | Down |
| C | 2 | 20 | Up |
| C | 3 | 39 | Down |
| C | 3 | 26 | Up |
| C | Empties | 52 | Down |
| C | Empties | 34 | Up |

These loads have been exceeded, and it was not unknown for the 5.55 p.m. goods to leave Calne with up to 50 empty wagons, whilst Jack Kington, signalman at Calne, remembers a special goods leaving on Christmas Day with no less than 86 empty wagons which ran through to Box. At this period of the war siding space at Calne was at a premium, and loaded wagons almost immediately filled any vacant siding space there.

Steam rail motors worked the branch from 1st February 1905. There were two steam railcars at Chippenham where the practice was to run them with a haycock fire, the fireman hoping his driver would be careful, and not shake the fire to pieces. Normally the railmotor was without a trailer in order to leave sufficient tractive power available to haul a Harris branded van. A steam railmotor carried a crew of driver, fireman and guard.

## LOCOMOTIVE SHEDS

The locomotive shed at Chippenham was a stone-walled, slated roof depot measuring 95ft by 50ft and built by Rowland Brotherhood, the Chippenham railway contractor. Opened circa 1858, it may have replaced, or incorporated, part of an earlier timber-built depot on the same site. The shed had three pits, each holding three 0-6-0PTs. A covered coaling stage was provided in 1938, but the coalman found it easier to throw coal from wagons straight into a locomotive bunker rather than use the coal crane, which lifted 10 cwt drums which had to be filled, wound up, the engine moved and the tub tipped into the bunker, with choking dust rising. Sometimes cleaners prepared ten tubs ready on the coal stage, whilst others found it more convenient to place the engine and coal wagon as close as possible to the point frog and shovel coal straight from wagon to bunker without using the tub. Railmotors had to be coaled from a wagon, as tubs would not fit through the doorway. Coal was stacked in their small bunker. Before 1926 there was a large coal stack beside the shed with 2,500 tons of coal. This was loaded up into wagons and removed during the 1926 Coal Strike. It was later replaced.

The sand furnace, of metal construction, was by the north-west corner of the shed. The cleaners or coalmen stoking the

furnace sometimes stole potatoes from a nearby field and roasted them on this furnace. Ashes were thrown out beside the pit and, when there was a good pile, were transferred to a wagon on the siding north-west of the shed to be taken away for disposal. The railmotor was stabled on this siding, put in about 1920. There was competition among cleaners to collect the wild strawberries which grew on the bank at the back of the shed. The 65ft diameter turntable was often used for turning the tender engines on trial runs from Swindon. When two cleaners were working the day shift, every three to four months they were required to take a very long-handled ring spanner and tighten any of the huge nuts which had worked loose on the table's centre boss. A steam pump for filling the water tank was situated in a road called Fogamshire, Bill Phillips the full-time pumper living in a company house on the opposite side of the road. If he was ill, the eldest cleaner took over, this job being very popular. It was replaced by an electric pump about 1938, and electrician and fitter coming from Swindon each week to maintain it. If the water dropped below a certain level, a bell rang in the engine shed until someone pressed a switch to cancel it and call the fitter, but as the tank gauge could be seen from the shed, someone was likely to notice it before the alarm bell sounded.

In 1918 there were about eight sets of men at the shed. During World War 2 the shed had 28 drivers, the same number of firemen, 5 cleaners, plus a chargeman responsible for rostering. One labourer on each shift coaled engines from wagons and cleaned the fires. There were three cleaners working nightly, one of whom was mainly occupied on callboy duties.

Calne engine shed, taken from the official survey, 26th January 1897.

# LOCOMOTIVES AND ROLLING STOCK

There was an endless transfer of footplate staff during the war years, some only stayed at Chippenham for a few weeks before being moved on elsewhere. About four men were made redundant after World War 2 due to the falling demand for ammunition. There were about 14 engines at Chippenham during World War 2 covering Calne branch workings, the government sidings at Thingley, trains to Farleigh Down ammunition sidings (Farleigh Down was the largest ammunition depot in Europe) and the ammunition depot in Box Tunnel. There were three sets of men at Thingley (one on each shift), three at Corsham, three at Farleigh and one each at Beanacre and Lacock. When the Malmesbury men had rest days, two men from Chippenham went to work the branch. In the post-war period the shed foreman was on duty from 7 a.m. to 3 p.m with the fire-dropper, coalman and cleaner, the chargehand supervising them at night. The cleaner on night duty cleaned below the footplate of the three engines, and then went round Chippenham knocking up the crews. One driver, very much a heavy sleeper, knowing that he could not be easily roused, tied a piece of string round his foot and dangled it through his bedroom window, the cleaner merely giving a wakening tug. Another driver insisted on having a call boy, but always opened the front door just as he was about to knock. this rather annoyed the cleaner who felt that his time had been wasted, so he tried to creep up without any warning and knock before the door opened, but never succeeded.

About six men were in the top link for auto working and, with others, made about 14 sets of men.

Chippenham was a sub-shed of Swindon and used the main shed's code: SDN in company days and later the BR code 82C. It closed on 2nd March 1964.

Calne shed opened with the branch in October 1863. The single road depot, with slated roof and stone walls measuring 30ft 2in by 21ft 10in, was capable of stabling one engine. It probably closed on the Calne Railway's amalgamation with the GWR, as on 26th January 1897 it was recorded that the shed had been out of use for many years. It was demolished in March 1906. Between the end of the platform and the shed stood a cast iron water tank, 20ft by 10ft by 5ft, its capacity at 4ft 6in deep being 5,625 gallons. At some period, the tank was replaced by that of a larger pattern, and a store room, latterly used for housing old records, occupied the base of the tank. A well, 13ft 6in deep with a diameter of 3ft 6in, was sited between this tank and the passenger platform, a pony walking round to work the 2-throw pump. This supply was disused by 1904, after which the tank was fed from Calne Water Works. The

0–4–2T No. 1433 standing at Chippenham in the late 1950s, with driver O. E. Britton and fireman John Archard in attendance. *K. Leech*

28ft 6in long, 8ft 6in wide, Siphon C No. 1496 built August 1910 to Diagram O9. The enamel plates were coloured chocolate and cream.
*M. Longridge*

Siphon C No. W1535 built 1907 to Diagram O8 (8ft width). The vehicle has a BR style roof board and GWR style plate on the side.
*Roye England*

# LOCOMOTIVES AND ROLLING STOCK

tank was not used for locomotive purposes for many years, at least not since 1939, but principally for supplying water to wash out the cattle pens. It was also used by the station staff as a swimming pool. Normally an engine had enough water to return to Chippenham, though if a driver was concerned and had an hour to spare, he unofficially took his engine to the cattle dock and put the pen washing hose into his tank.

## COACHES

The first electrically lit coaches to run on the branch appeared on an excursion circa 1922. They were hauled by an 0-6-0 Dean Goods, which returned late in the evening and, after dropping about 60 passengers at Black Dog, failed to start on the 1 in 100 rising gradient and had to reverse for about a quarter of a mile to get a run.

The Marquess of Lansdowne had a first class compartment in auto coach No. 13 and, if he was not occupying it, permitted it to be used by other passengers if their's was full. Auto coaches were gas lit and between 1950–60 were gradually changed to electric lighting. Coaches were recharged at the New-Found-Out siding, Chippenham, the gas tank wagon returning to the railway gas works at Swindon for re-gassing. Passenger coaches were examined daily by one of the three carriage and wagon examiners at Chippenham. There were two carriage cleaners at Chippenham responsible for the Calne stock – three auto trailers, two in use and one kept as spare on the New-Found-Out – and coaches used on the Trowbridge branch. No. 45, an example of an auto coach with a corridor connection at its trailing end, worked on the Calne branch in 1952.

## VANS

A feature of the Calne branch for much of its life was the Harris' branded Siphon vans despatched from Calne to many parts of the country. Two types were used: the 4-wheel Siphon C and the bogie Siphon F. In brown livery, they carried enamel roof boards with black lettering on a yellow ground stating the destination, such as 'Harris (Calne) Wiltshire Sausages, Calne to Newcastle', the destination being repeated about halfway up the van side. Messrs. Harris paid for the display of these enamel signs which were cleaned daily by a Chippenham

A Siphon G built in 1930, for fruit and vegetables and converted to ambulance train use in 1940, hence the shell vents and heating which were retained after World War II. This photo was taken at Calne in September 1964. *D. J. Hyde*

Harris branded bogie Siphon F built in 1906 to Diagram O7 and shown here in BR livery. The enamel plates had white letters on a red ground. Notice the gas tanks slung below the floor.
*Roye England*

carriage cleaner who travelled on the 1.53 p.m. ex Chippenham and returned on the 5.0 p.m. Harris' traffic manager periodically checked that they had been cleaned. Bogie Siphon Gs were used on Sundays. At Calne a goods engine shunted the empty Siphons into the end of the passenger platform and, after loading, the auto engine was buffered up to them for coupling. They were taken as tail traffic to Chippenham, where they were removed by the down side pilot and placed on the appropriate train, though if the van was through to Portsmouth, it travelled as far as Westbury with the Westbury auto. A gas tank wagon was kept in the side platform, pipes running across to the Siphons which were fitted with gas lighting. One of the Chippenham carriage and wagon examiners came over and checked the Siphons and other types of vehicle. When wartime circumstances caused a shortage of Siphons, sausages were loaded into passenger coaches and transferred to vans at Chippenham.

## DIESELS

On 5th October 1958 DMUs began working the majority of branch trips. On Sundays to Fridays, the centre trailer was removed from the Derby 3-car suburban set (later Class 116) to enable the two power cars to tow the sausage vans. The set ran light from Dr Day's Sidings, Bristol, early every morning, returning after the last branch trip at night. At one period the DMU was stabled overnight on School Siding, Chippenham. The driver was then required to check the engines, and start each separately from the ground, allowing them to warm the coaches. The engines were then switched off and re-started from the driver's cab. One roster involved booking on in the afternoon, relieving at Chippenham the driver of the 4.10 p.m. from Swindon; working to Bristol Temple Meads and Weston-super-Mare; then back to Dr Day's, picking up a fresh DMU and working the last train from Temple Meads to Chippenham, putting the DMU in a siding and locking it, leaving it ready for a man the next morning to work two trips to Calne; to Box and back; then to Bristol. The Calne branch was not operated as a shuttle service, a train from Westbury covering the middle part of the day. In addition to the Derby suburban type DMUs, Gloucester C & WW and Swindon Cross Country Units (later classes 119 and 120) also appeared.

Goods trains were handled by 0-6-0, Type 1 D95XX 650 h.p. diesel-hydraulics and D20XX diesel mechanicals (later Class 03), the latter being restricted to twelve loaded wagons. One travelled so slowly between Stanley and Hazeland Bridge that it is said that the guard was able to jump off, pick a handful of nuts and berries and climb back into his van again.

BR introduced a four-character train identification system for diesels, the first character indicating the class of train. For passengers trains, the second character indicated the area, those to Calne bearing a 'B' for Bristol. The last two characters indicated the destination:

*Chippenham–Calne*
33 for important trains (former Class A headcode)
83 for local trains (former Class B and empty coaching stock, formerly Class C)
73 was for local trains Trowbridge–Westbury.

Due to the limitations of a two-panel display, Code B2 usually appeared on the branch passenger trains.

For local freight and light engines, the last three characters indicated the destination, the Calne branch being C10.

Two Pressed Steel single unit motor brake seconds, with tail traffic of two vans, on the 11.00 a.m. Sunday train from Calne to Chippenham. This picture was taken near Calne fixed distant. *D. Lovelock*

# CHAPTER SIX
# PERMANENT WAY AND SIGNALLING

DETAILS of the original permanent way were given in the Board of Trade inspecting officer's report. The Calne branch was relaid with second-hand 30ft rail, later replaced by 'oo' rail from the Severn Tunnel in 45ft lengths. On the curve at Cocklebury where the branch left the main line, the check rail wore thin with the wheel flanges grinding against it. In 1930 the GWR ordered 136,000 experimental steel sleepers, some being used on the Calne branch below Studley and others for half a mile from Black Dog siding towards Calne. The permanent way gang found it was more difficult keeping the correct level and cant with these rather than the wooden type, because problems were experienced with packing. An early BR mechanical tamper was tried, but was unable to cope with the steel sleepers and did more harm than good.

The permanent way gang based at Calne in a timber-built permanent way cabin, consisted of nine to ten men. They started work at 7 a.m. and finished at 5 p.m., working 7–12 on Saturdays. They had a push trolley which was kept in the open at Calne. Each morning the ganger walked the line from Calne to Chippenham taking about three hours. If the gang was working, say, at Black Dog, Edward Culley, ganger, might walk from Calne to Black Dog, catch a train to Chippenham and then walk back to Black Dog. On a hot day he walked his length again in the afternoon to check that the rail joints had not closed due to expansion. The gang's daily work involved packing, drainage work and fencing. Frank Stapleford was the only man in the gang capable of using a hand scythe and it took him six months to work his way from Calne to Chippenham and back. The hay was sold to farmers. The permanent way was kept well, the gang gaining the annual prize for the best kept length in the Bristol Division on more than one occasion.

Between Calne and Studley there were several slips – at Keevil's cattle creep and the west end of Calne yard; the Sewage Slip, opposite the sewage farm west of Black Dog; and the site of the canal bridge at the top of Stanley bank. Once a week ballast had to be put under sleepers at these places to keep the line level. Ash ballast was used in the sidings at Calne and on the slips, but they gradually went over to stone. Ash ballast was laid in weak places as it made for easier lifting for packing and also put less weight on weak embankments.

The permanent way men were paid a shilling extra if off their own length for meal time, so if the Chippenham gang went on the Calne branch to unload ballast, the foreman took the gang and train back to Chippenham for lunch, rather than on to Calne, in order to avoid paying the shilling. The Chippenham gang also helped with track relaying on the branch. During the winter half of the year when the Severn Tunnel was closed on Sundays, the Calne permanent way gang worked there.

Permanent way men availed themselves of the opportunity of catching rabbits and one driver, 'Bristol Jack', collected them as he passed, from a stick held up by permanent way men, using the skill he had gained collecting tokens.

The present permanent way office at Chippenham was the original refreshment room before replacements were opened on the up and down platforms.

## SIGNALLING
Chippenham West box was closed 2.30 p.m.–5.0 p.m. Sundays and 12.50 a.m.–6.0 a.m. Mondays. It contained 27 levers, including 6 spares. Chippenham East box, open continuously, had 64 levers, 9 of which were spare. The lineman, whose cabin was situated behind the East box, maintained routes to Calne, Dauntsey, Corsham and Lacock, aided by his assistant lineman and two lineman's lads. The Calne branch was worked with a train staff, which was red and square in shape, and one engine in steam. There was no intermediate block post. When Black Dog siding opened, this was worked by Annett's key. Black Dog ground frame had two levels, the second siding not being worked from the frame. Latterly the branch was worked by electric train token. When DMUs worked over the branch, the electric train token was exchanged at Chippenham through an auxiliary electric token instrument situated at the London end of the down platform, the guard either collecting it from the driver and taking it to the instrument, or vice versa. This was to avoid damage to windows or coach bodywork if exchanged near the signal box. An emergency staff was available if the regular staff became lost.

One driver of an up train shunting at Black Dog, on arrival at Chippenham could not find the tablet. It had been removed from the large loop which aided catching, in order that it could be used to unlock the ground frame. It was the shunter's custom to place the tablet on the sandbox after he had taken it from the frame, so that the fireman could return it to the loop and hang it in the cab. As it could not be found, pilotman working had to be instituted. The driver, now off duty, realised that the fireman had failed to take the tablet from the sandbox and that it had probably dropped off en route from Black Dog. He then set off walking back along the line hoping to find it, but all to no avail. When the next driver of the engine was inspecting the locomotive following its arrival at Calne, he found the missing tablet lodged beneath the bunker.

At one period the engine of the first goods train from Chippenham to Calne returned to Chippenham attached to the front of the 9.0 a.m. auto, the goods engine heading the train while the auto driver worked his engine from the vestibule.

This regular imbalance of movements over the branch resulted in a continued accumulation of tablets at Calne, so approximately once a month the signalman at Chippenham East advised when he had only about half a dozen tablets left, and the lineman had to move tokens from Calne to Chippenham East.

As the signalman at Chippenham East had to walk about 25 yards to the token post, to save his legs he usually received the tablet by hand from the fireman, or sometimes the fireman threw it on the ground.

In order to avoid the necessity of verbally advising the Chippenham East signalman of shunting operations required

# THE CALNE BRANCH

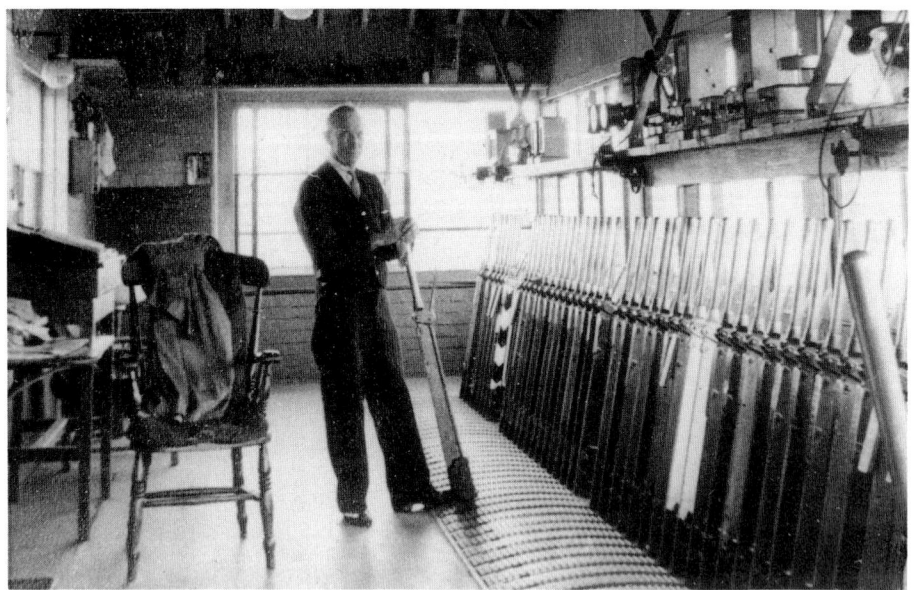

Signalman Walter Eggleton in Chippenham East signal box c.1953, leaning on the facing point lock lever for the Calne branch. *R. Ball*

to be carried out at the east end of Chippenham down platform, the station foreman was in bell communication with him using the following code:

| Message | Number of beats | How to be given |
| --- | --- | --- |
| Call attention | 1 | |
| Close points | 2 | Consecutively |
| Train or vehicles on down line for down siding | 3 | Consecutively |
| Train or vehicles in down siding for down line | 3 | 1 pause 2 |
| Train or vehicles on down line for spur | 4 | Consecutively |
| Train or vehicles in spur for down line | 4 | 2 pause 2 |
| Engine or vehicles from spur to bay or vice versa | 4 | 3 pause 1 |
| Close spur catch point | 4 | 1 pause 3 |
| Engine or vehicles from spur to bay siding or vice versa | 6 | 3 pause 3 |
| Engine or vehicles to cross from down line to up line | 5 | Consecutively |
| Engine or vehicles required to propel up the down line | 7 | 2 pause 5 |
| Obstruction Danger | 6 | Consecutively |

It was stipulated that the 'Call Attention' signal must precede all other signals, except 'Obstruction Danger'; the signalman was required to repeat the bells if the requested movement could be made and, until correctly returned, the station staff were forbidden to make that movement. Movements were not permitted with coaches containing passengers. Immediately vehicles were detached from a passenger train at Chippenham, the person concerned was required to switch the track circuit to 'Vehicle on Line' and maintain it there until their removal. In addition, he was required to inform the signalman what it was intended to do with them.

This special code caused confusion to one signalman at Chippenham East circa 1950. With a 14XX class 0-4-2 tank engine and two auto cars stood in the down siding, he set the road for it to move to the down platform and pulled the signal off. Time elapsed and he heard two bells which he believed came from the station foreman indicating 'Close points'. Had he distinguished the different tone he could have realised the bells code really came from Chippenham West signal box and indicated 'Train on Line'. Believing that he was instructed to close the points, he did so, just as the front bogie of the leading auto car had gone out on to the main line. His movement meant that the rest of the train proceeded towards the Fish Dock. Luckily the auto train crew became aware of the situation and applied the brakes. Although the car was not derailed, the auto gear was strained and the vehicle had to be taken out of service.

Electric train tokens for diesel trains working over the Calne branch were exchanged at Chippenham through the Auxiliary Electric Token Instrument situated at the London end of the down platform. As soon as a branch train arrived, the guard was required to obtain the token from the driver and insert it in the Auxiliary Electric Token Instrument, turn the token, afterwards withdrawing and lowering it into either column of the magazine. The guard of a departing train was required to collect a token from the instrument and convey it to the driver. When the signalman at Chippenham East Signal box needed to release a token from the Auxiliary Token Instrument, he sent 'Is Line Clear?' signal to Calne signal box and on receiving 'Line Clear', both signalmen pressed plungers to release the token from the auxiliary instrument.

To accept a train under Regulation 4, the Chippenham East signalman needed a clear line at least a quarter mile ahead of his home signal. This meant that if, when the Calne signalman offered a train, he could not guarantee that a train on the down line would be clear of Chippenham station, he would reply with 2-2-2, thus indicating 'Line clear to clearing point only'. In acknowledgement the Calne signalman repeated 2-2-2 and, as the train left Calne, to indicate that the road was only clear to the home signal, he displayed a green flag, or green light, to the driver who responded with a whistle.

If there was an extra long main line down goods at Chippenham and the following train wished to pass, the Calne branch was used as a siding until the main line was clear.

In addition to being important for signalling, when signalman Albert Ball was on duty, Chippenham East box was an important centre for solving work problems, he being the local secretary of the National Union of Railwaymen. He also held the same office for the Local Departmental Committee, the latter being set up by management to iron out problems. Many men of all ranks from porter to station master came to the box to have their difficulties solved.

Worked on two shifts, Calne signal box was opened daily at the start, and closed at the end of the train service. Early turn began about 5.45 a.m. when the signalman switched in the box and allowed Chippenham East to withdraw the token. Early duty lasted until 1.45 p.m. when the late turn took over and continued until the last train from Calne reached Chippenham. All signalmen working there held keys to the box. The 16 lever frame (4 spares) was unusual in that the levers were not in line, those in the centre being two to three inches forward of the four or five at each end. Each sliding window in the box originally had nine panes, but about 1962 the more modern pattern, three small panes above and two larger below, were fitted.

The platform road at Calne had to be clear before a train could be accepted from Chippenham. When vans were against the stops at the far end of the platform, a train was accepted under Regulation 5 – a warning arrangement. If Chippenham East rang 3-1-3 asking the road for an auto, and if vans were at the platform, Calne would return 3-5-5. As the train passed Chippenham East box, the signalman displayed a green hand signal using a flag or lamp, the driver acknowledging with a whistle. Having received confirmation that the warning was understood, he lowered the branch starter so that the train could proceed to Calne. The Calne signalman kept his home on until the driver 'blew up', then lowered it in order to allow the train to enter the platform. During darkness, fog, or falling snow, the leading vehicle on the platform road was required to display a red light towards Chippenham and each train had to be piloted from the home signal by a competent man appointed by the station master.

**Signalman Albert Ball, 4th December 1966.** *R. Ball*

The down home signal carried a bracket arm allowing access to the goods yard, and similarly access to the run-round loop from the platform road, was indicated by a bracket signal attached to the up main starter, that is until about 1960 when it was replaced by a ground disc. The only track circuit at Calne was in the rear of the down home signal.

In order to avoid stopping at Calne signal box, a DMU driver retained the tablet until he had brought the train to a stand at the proper place at the platform, the signalman then collecting it from him. The signalman was required to personally convey the token to the driver of an up train. Following the closure of Calne signal box, from 2nd November 1964 'one engine in steam' working was re-introduced.

**The staff used on the branch following the removal of the sidings at Calne, when 'one engine in steam' working was in operation.** *Author*

0–4–2T No. 1400 with two auto coaches at Calne.

Author's Collection

# CHAPTER SEVEN
# RUN DOWN AND CLOSURE

ALTHOUGH times varied slightly, the following is typical of the years 1945–1951.

5.45 a.m. Chippenham–Calne goods with K headlights. 57XX hauled. The engine stayed at Calne shunting for most of the day. Pannier tank engines always faced Bristol – this was convenient for shunting at Chippenham where the shunter was always on the driver's side.

6.10 am Chippenham–Calne auto 14XX. The 14XX class always worked chimney facing Swindon so that the coach was at the terminal end of the Calne bay at Chippenham. Two auto cars were the usual make-up.

6.35 am Auto from Calne. Passengers were mainly workers for Westinghouse. This train was poorly timed as workers there did not have to clock in until 7.30.

7.5 am Chippenham–Calne auto. A dozen workers for Harris arrived on this.

7.25 am Calne–Box auto. (This returned as the 8.25 Box–Chippenham.)

8.5 am Chippenham–Calne mixed train.

8.25 am Calne–Chippenham, mainly schoolchildren and Westinghouse clerks. B set Calne–Bristol Temple Meads via Melksham and Bradford on Avon.

8.48 am Chippenham–Calne. (The auto returning from Box. It used the up main platform at Chippenham.)

9.5 am Calne–Chippenham auto. Mostly shoppers. Then followed a layover for the engine which went to the Calne spur. (At 10.20 a.m. it worked the Chippenham–Westbury.)

10.30 am Chippenham–Calne, a B set from Bath with a 55XX and worked by Bath men. Through working from up main.

10.50 am Calne–Chippenham B set and 55XX. (On arrival at Chippenham it was shunted into the Weymouth bay and went forward at 11.50 a.m. to Bristol Temple Meads.)

11.15 am Saturdays only goods Chippenham–Calne, K class, Pannier.

11.48 am Chippenham–Calne auto. (This was the Chippenham auto which had returned with the 11.10 a.m. Trowbridge–Calne, a through working which used the up main platform.)

12.20 pm Calne–Chippenham auto.

12.50 pm Chippenham–Calne auto.

1.7 pm Calne–Chippenham. (On Wednesdays this train was crowded with people going to Bath for shopping.) On arrival at Chippenham the auto car went to the Calne bay and the engine to shed.

1.50 pm Chippenham–Calne. (This was a through train Bristol Temple Meads to Calne which left at 12.25 p.m. It consisted of two B sets

2–6–2T No. 5566 with the 1.12 p.m. Saturdays only Calne to Weston-super-Mare c.1951.   *M. E. J. Deane*

0—4—2T No. 1436 with the 10.30 a.m. Sundays only ex-Chippenham, running into Calne with nine vans of pigs. *D. Lovelock*

hauled by a 55XX or 82XXX in later days, worked by Bristol Bath Road men. This train used the up main platform.)

2.20 pm Calne–Chippenham. The above train returning.

2.35 pm Saturdays excepted, Chippenham–Calne goods, K class lights, Pannier hauled.

2.40 pm Saturdays only, Calne–Chippenham goods. (The return of the 11.15 am.)

2.55 pm Saturdays only, Chippenham–Calne auto.

3.15 pm Saturdays only, Calne–Chippenham auto.

4.30 pm Chippenham–Calne crowded with schoolchildren. (This was the Westbury auto with a 54XX engine working the 3.50 p.m. Trowbridge–Calne.)

5.0 pm Calne–Chippenham. (The return of the above.)

5.20 pm Chippenham–Calne with Westinghouse clerks. (The above train.)

5.35 pm Calne–Westbury with Harris' tail traffic.

6.35 pm Chippenham–Calne. Pannier and MELON coach from the fish bay. Behind the coach were often trucks of live pigs, Siphon Cs, SR utility vans and horse-boxes.

7.5 pm Calne–Chippenham worked by the above, with Harris' tail traffic. On arrival coach stabled in fish bay.

8.30 pm Chippenham–Calne 14XX and auto coach. (This was the 7.25 p.m. ex Trowbridge. At Chippenham it was shunted from the up main to the Calne bay.)

9.0 pm Calne–Chippenham auto.

9.30 pm Chippenham–Calne auto.

10.5 pm Calne–Chippenham auto.

11.00 pm Wednesdays and Saturdays only, Chippenham–Calne auto.

11.20 pm Wednesdays and Saturdays only, Calne–Chippenham auto.

An arrival at Chippenham of the last train from Calne the auto car was stabled in the Calne bay and the engine went to shed.

## PASSENGER TRAIN OPERATION

Usually there were no more than two coaches on the auto, but if a third was added, it would be attached to the front of the engine, as the regulator could not be operated through the rodding of three vehicles. In fact, because of the slack, it could not always be done on two, but the rattle of the regulator when the driver was trying to move it from his remote compartment, indicated to the fireman left on the engine that he should open it. Because an auto train fireman had to be capable of working unsupervised, he was required to be a passed fireman.

A length of string coupled the whistle wire between the auto coach and the engine. This was a primitive safety device, but as it was easy to forget to uncouple it when a locomotive was being detached, it would at least break whereas wire would have been pulled right out. When a non-auto train arrived at Calne, the engine had to run round to the other end of the train, a procedure made a little more time-consuming as the train had to be reversed along the platform first due to the position of the run-round loop.

Although an auto train driver was able to apply the brake from his vestibule, he was unable to release it, so when the guard gave a single 'Start' ring on the bell, the driver responded with two rings which rang in the engine cab and indicated 'Blow off brake'. The fireman then opened the ejector to create a vacuum to release the brakes. When the gauge showed the required reading, the fireman gave a single blast on the whistle to warn of the train's departure and, providing that the driver's gauge agreed, he opened the regulator from his vestibule.

In the season, less patronised auto trains unofficially stopped by Bowood Estate, where the crew climbed down to cut bean sticks beside the line. After spending some time doing this, they sped quickly to Calne breaking the branch limit of 30 mph. More sticks were cut on the return trip and the bundle brought back to Chippenham. Passing the Bowood Estate, the occasional pheasant was sometimes struck and might be picked up off the front of the engine. Game was particularly attracted to the line if a bag of grain had leaked and its contents trickled on the track.

Working the line generally gave no problems to the locomotive crew, a boiler of water taking a train two-thirds of the way along the branch even with a heavy load.

On Saturday evenings during World War 2 there were usually many servicemen on the last train and it was common practice for it not to stop at Black Dog on the down journey, otherwise intoxicated members of the armed forces would get off, thinking it was Calne, and the guard would experience difficulty getting them on board again. To avoid this problem, it was the custom to tell local residents who wanted to get off at Black Dog that they would be carried through the Calne and dropped off on the return to Chippenham. Guards always had to be on the look-out for unsuspecting servicemen at Black Dog, as Stanley Bridge Halt was the only intermediate stop in the timetable so they assumed the stop after Stanley Bridge must be Calne. Two lady guards worked the branch during the war, Joan Smith, the youngest in Britain, and Peggy May.

Guards called out 'Any one for Stanley Halt?' and if there was no reply, gave one ring of the electric bell on the auto trailer so that the driver would know that there was no need to stop unless a passenger was waiting on the platform. In the absence of corridor connections, the guard could only carry out this practice if the train consisted of a single car. The electric bell sounded in the driver's vestibule and on the engine. No flags were used by the auto train guard, the bell sufficed. The simple code set out in the 1936 General Appendix to the Rule Book:

| 1 ring | To start |
| 2 rings | Fireman blow off brake |
| 3 rings | To stop |

was later modified to:

| 1 ring | Stop |
| 2 rings | Start |
| 3 rings | Set back |
| 3–3 rings | Guard required by driver |
| 4 rings | Slow down when propelling |
| 5 rings | Guard leaving train in accordance with Rules |
| 6 rings | Draw forward |

In winter the guard was required to light lamps at Stanley Bridge Halt at dusk and extinguish them on the last run at

'2251' class 0–6–0 No. 2203 from Swindon shed, at Black Dog Halt with an engineer's train, in the late 1950s. A tender engine was used on these trains to avoid any shortage of water.  *D. Lovelock*

night. Although officially it was the guard's duty, the fireman would often put out the one near the engine in order to save time.

The guard's vestibule in an auto trailer contained a metal rack for storing destination boards and a locked used ticket box divided into three sections, each with a slot. Guards used their own classification, such as the left slot for single tickets, the centre for returns and the right for 'off line tickets' that is, those originating beyond the Calne branch. The box was unlocked and cleared at Chippenham. The guard obtained a black box containing new tickets from Chippenham booking office, the tickets being kept in a bus conductor style rack. Cash collected in a strong cloth pouch was paid in to Chippenham booking office. Tickets were sold to passengers boarding at Stanley Bridge and also to those at Black Dog at times when the porter in charge of the latter was off duty. Because of the crowds of servicemen returning from leave using the last Sunday train, two Calne leading porters collected tickets en route to avoid the need for a late ticket collector at Calne.

Leaving the bay platform at Chippenham the 'Calne Bunk', as it was popularly called, took the up main line and then crossed over the down main to the Calne branch. On returning,

Empty cattle vans after being smashed against the blocks by a goods train on 18th May 1955. The goods office can be seen above the gate to the cattle pens and Harris's loading bay on the right. *D. Lovelock and Mrs. P. Gleed*

it followed the down main, unloaded, shunted back into the 'Calne Spur' and then moved forward into the Calne bay. A cordon (a gas wagon, of lateral or longitudinal pattern) was kept in a siding called the New-Found-Out beside the Calne bay. Replenished at the railway gas works, Swindon, it was used for rcharging the gas-lit auto coaches.

## TRAIN OPERATIONS

Goods trains to Calne were really limited to 25 wagons, the maximum capacity of the run-round loop. Before a down freight was allowed to enter the sidings at Calne, the signalman was required to obtain permission from the shunter, or in his absence, check that the siding was clear and the hand points were correctly set to the train's destination. The signal controlling the entrance to the siding was not to be lowered until the train had been brought almost to a stand. Then it was turned into the goods yard. When stopped clear of the points, the driver blew three whistles and the guard waved to the signalman, who then restored the road. The shunter or fireman uncoupled the engine which then ran over on to the platform road and reversed to the opposite end of the loop. The signalman then displayed a green hand-lamp for the engine to run forwards to the brake van, then once again the driver blew three blasts on the whistle to indicate that it was clear of the running road so the signalman could shut the engine in the goods yard so that shunting could commence and not interfere with another train working to Calne.

After a pig train passed Black Dog Halt, it was the practice for the driver to sound the 'pig whistle', that is, the brake whistle, so by the time he reached Calne, Harris's lorries were waiting to collect the animals. Originally, livestock was driven on hoof between station and factory.

It was not unknown for a train to come to a standstill on the gradient between Black Dog and Calne, and have to be divided. As Calne was situated at the summit of a gradient of 1 in 110, great care had to be exercised in shunting vehicles to and from the running line, an engine always being at the Chippenham end of vehicles shunted. In the event of any requirement to stand vehicles temporarily on the main line without an engine attached, the wheels of the two wagons nearest Chippenham were required to be spragged in addition to the hand brakes on these and any other wagons being put down and tightly secured. When necessary, not more than eight vehicles (not exceeding 36 wheels) were allowed to stand at the platform line dead end, the leading wheels securely scotched in addition to hand brakes being tightly secured.

At Chippenham the Westinghouse Brake & Signal Company's private siding, known as Pew Hill Siding, branched off the Running & Maintenance shed road and was worked by a two-lever ground frame, locked by Annett's key, interlocked with Chippenham East signal box. When the siding was required to be used, the shunter informed the signalman who could release the Annett's key, for the shunter to unlock the ground frame. Westinghouse shunted wagons within the siding using a red Fordson agricultural tractor fitted with buffers. Following its sale in 1978, until the siding was closed in 1982, wagons were shunted by a fork-lift truck fitted with a buffer bar.

The points leading to Chippenham Gas Works siding and the wheel stop were required to be unlocked when traffic was being shunted to or from the siding, the keys being kept in Chippenham East box. When loaded wagons were being shunted into the siding they had to be coupled to the engine until brought to a stand and not pushed over the weighbridge. the number of wagons dealt with at any one time was restricted to four. The shunter was responsible for the safe working of the siding and seeing that the points and wheel stop were locked and the keys returned to the signal box.

In the winter 1954–5 thirteen trains ran each way plus a mid-afternoon train on Saturdays and a late train Wednesdays and Saturdays. Most were autos. Six trains ran each way on Sundays. There was one down mixed train on weekdays, but no corresponding up mixed working. Two goods trains ran each way daily. Three years later the timetable was similar, but there was one extra train daily including Sundays.

In the 1950s the 12.54 p.m. ex Calne with eight coaches ran through to Weston-super-Mare carrying express headlights. It really acted as a relief to the 1.0 p.m. Swindon to Bristol which followed it from Chippenham. At one period it consisted of about six ex-LMS coaches and, on at least three occasions circa 1950, included two air-conditioned coaches from the 'Coronation Scot'. Originating from Swindon, it was often headed by a sparkling locomotive ex works. Early in World War 2, before the passenger platform was lengthened, this train departed from the cattle dock. Troop trains of ten or more coaches in length, also departed from here. In 1948–9 the through train to Weston-super-Mare was hauled by a 57XX class 0-6-0 PT from Chippenham shed worked by Chippenham men from the Second Link.

A spectacular accident happened at Calne on 18th May 1955 after a shunter had placed cattle trucks in the pig siding and failed to re-set the points for the loop. When the goods train arrived, its driver, seeing the road incorrectly set, applied his brakes more firmly, but the wheels locked. the train continued, striking the cattle wagons and causing £7,000 worth of damage, though the only harm to the engine was two broken bricks in the firebox arch.

In 1953 it was quite usual for the two auto trailers to have a total of 150 passengers. At times trains were so crowded that passengers stood in the luggage compartment. In the early 1950s passengers arriving at, or departing from, Calne numbered about 300,000 a year, that is about a thousand daily. In the twelve months ending 3th September 1952, the branch claimed a revenue of £150,000. Statistics were:

300,000 incoming and outgoing passengers
500,000 packages despatched from Calne by passenger train
About 10,000 wagons handled
Over 7,000 weighings on weighbridge
Over 200 special passenger trains.

By 1959 figures had declined:

98,000 booked passengers incoming and outgoing
200,000 passengers in total.
171,000 outwards parcels
35,000 inwards parcels
6,000 tons outwards freight
16,000 tons inwards freight.

The 1955 ASLEF strike marked the beginning of the end of the Harris traffic when more and more was transferred to the road. Coach operators gradually creamed off traffic from the RAF camps, a full coach being run to London and another to Manchester. The railway staff pleaded with management for

# 106 THE CALNE BRANCH

the issue of weekend tickets, but the idea was not accepted. Then, when nearly all the traffic had been lost, weekend tickets were issued and, though very competitive, came too late. Management was not realistic – negotiations were in progress to win a bulk fertiliser contract between ICI and a local agricultural merchant. This would have involved building a ramp at Calne below track level so that fertiliser could flow from truck to lorry, but the idea was dismissed as too expensive.

When Chippenham swimming pool opened, many users travelled by rail from Calne – stimulated by a local promotion.

A blank poster depicting a football was issued to stations so that times of trains to matches could be inserted, but ingenious Calne staff wrote: 'Football in Australia – but go to Chippenham for the Swimming.'

With dieselisation, the summer of 1959 saw a complicated timetable with quite a number of different timings on Saturdays and offering more first and second class trains. Seven each way were run on Sundays. The summer of 1961 saw seventeen each way on weekdays plus one on Wednesdays; seven on Sundays, six of these running after 5 p.m. to cater for ser-

A '94XX' class 0–6–0PT near Black Dog Halt with the 2.20 p.m. Calne–Chippenham. This was one of the few trains over the branch which had first class accommodation. As this was a 'red' engine, it was officially forbidden to work over the branch.
*D. Lovelock*

BR Standard Class 3 2–6–2T No. 82007 (shedded at Bristol, Bath Road) crossing the A4 trunk road at Black Dog with the 10.22 a.m. Chippenham to Calne.
*D. Lovelock*

# RUN DOWN AND CLOSURE

The curved roof of Harris's hangar can be seen to the right of the goods shed. The two buildings on the far right are Harris's by-products factory. The air raid shelter on the left was used as the station foreman's hut.
*Lens of Sutton*

vicemen returning to camp. In 1962 traffic had fallen sufficiently to cut back several daytime and late evening services to offer fourten each way plus two on Saturdays. All Sunday trains were withdrawn on 5th March 1962.

Around this time driver Frank Cannon was in charge of a DMU when it struck a branch which had fallen across the line near the advanced home signal at Chippenham. It had brought down telegraph wires which had caught under the DMU.

Immediately after the blizzard of 27th December 1962, Driver Cannon was given a tank engine to see if he could make his way through to Calne, but he was stopped by drifts and, after several attempts, had to return to Chippenham defeated. On 30th December a Hymek diesel fitted with a snow plough was sent from Bristol, special dispensation being given as this class of locomotive was normally banned from working over the branch. Driver Cannon acted as pilot to the Hymek's Bristol driver who did not know the road. At Glass's Crossing (1 mile 20 ch) between Chippenham and Stanley Bridge, snow came right to the top of the cutting. One drift was on the Chippenham side of Stanley Bridge Halt and when the plough appeared, people came out of the waiting shelter to watch the operation, but as soon as they saw the snow being pushed towards them, quickly scattered before they were smothered. The DMU did not run for several days, but the platform inspector at Chippenham contacted Control to ask if passengers could travel in the brake van of the steam-hauled goods train. Control agreed as long as the guard gave his assent, which he did, realising that otherwise the Harris commuters would have been unable to get to work. Passengers from Calne, mainly Westinghouse workers, travelled to Chippenham standing in a Siphon. Later in the day, coaches were obtained for steam-powered services over the branch.

A DMU, seen on trial at Calne.
*Clive Gale*

## CLOSURE

By late 1963 only one freight train ran each weekday, with just full truckloads running through to Calne. Small consignments were dealt with by Chippenham. The last RAF leave special ran on 28th May 1963 and was made up of eight coaches. It was unusual that passenger services outlived those of freight as in the mid-sixties it was often the reverse. Freight services were withdrawn on 2nd November, the last train running on 31st October hauled by 0-6-0 D2186 (later 03 class). Calne signal box was closed and thereafter the station was only staffed until 2 pm, guards issuing tickets after this time and advising the

108 THE CALNE BRANCH

0-6-0DM D2186 leaving Calne on 31st October 1963 with the last freight train. *D. Lovelock*

Another view of the last freight train leaving Calne with goods guard Monty Fell leaning out of the brake van. Although the last goods train was to have run on Friday, it would have been grossly overloaded, so the final run was made on Saturday, 31st October 1964. This view at Keevil's Crossing shows the headshunt stop block. *D. Lovelock*

signalman at Chippenham East when a train was ready for departure.

Following the publication of the 1963 Beeching Report, which recommended the closing of the Calne branch, a Joint Consultation Meeting between BR management and staff was held on 13th August 1964. The accountants' financial statement attributed an income of £6,300 to the line, whereas staff claimed that relevant passenger receipts for the branch were in the region of £17,000. Management replied that the £6,300 was revenue 'directly attributable to that portion of journeys over the branch', and added that receipts had declined over the last three years. Management also observed that, because for a number of years the Calne branch had been thought likely to close, maintenance work had been withheld and, if the line was to be retained, a complete track relaying programme would be necessary and some of the bridges required attention. Staff believed that the line could have been economically worked by a 2-car DMU with two drivers and two guards and that Calne station should have been unstaffed, but the management felt the branch would still have been uneconomic and revenue would not have equalled movements cost. Based on the 1964 service expenses would have been:

Power car + driving trailer and no staff at Calne –
  Movement cost    £10,118 p.a
  Terminal cost    £ 1,000 p.a
  i.e. an income of   £11,118    against a revenue of £6,300.

Power car only and no staff at Calne –
  Movement cost    £8,735
  Terminal cost    £1,000
  i.e. an income of   £9,735    against a revenue of £6,300

Timetable for the period 10th September 1962 to 16th June 1963.

A 3-car DMU on the 1.0 p.m. Calne–Chippenham, crossing the Avon at Black Bridge on 4th September 1965. *Hugh Ballantyne*

Another DMU, with flanges squealing round the check-railed curve at Calne Junction, on 9th September 1965. *P. Strong*

The last Sundays only 11.00 a.m. to Chippenham leaving Calne on 12th September 1965. It is a Swindon 3-car cross-country DMU with a bogie van as tail traffic. The bracketed disc signalled access to the goods yard.    *D. Lovelock*

Each of the above costings took the full debit of permanent way, building and signalling expenses.

Management said that every endeavour had been made to obtain traffic for the branch, even to the extent of appealing to local traders to patronise the services, but this effort had met with a very poor response.

A census during the week ending 10th October 1964 revealed that the average number of passengers per train alighting at Calne or Chippenham was about thirteen, Stanley Bridge and Black Dog halts only having about half a dozen passengers daily.

A staff suggestion received in March 1965 was that the 6.05 a.m. Chippenham to Calne passenger train be retimed to depart from Chippenham at 6.30 p.m. since it did not leave Calne until 7.05. The person who suggested the amendment believed an economy could be made by later booking on times of the passenger guard, driver, booking clerk at Chippenham, and porter at Calne. He pointed out that the train only carried one or two passengers, two bundles of newspapers for Black Dog Halt which were not collected until 7.30 a.m. and an empty wages cash box. Management said that four regular passengers travelled on the DMU, and an alteration of time would not allow savings to be made on the train diagram.

Another staff suggestion received was that a rail bus should be employed and run through to Bath and Swindon. Management turned down this suggestion as a rail bus could not have coped with peak hour loadings of 54 passengers, and an Unremunerative Railway Services investigation had revealed that there was little demand for additional through facilities.

The Minister of Transport, Tom Fraser, gave his consent to closure subject to adequate provision being made to augment the existing bus services. In addition to the existing 22 buses run each way, another five were added. Through rail services at the time of withdrawal were:

| | |
|---|---|
| 08.26 | Calne – Bristol Temple Meads |
| 13.00 | Calne – Westbury |
| 17.32 | Calne – Westbury |
| 21.35 | Calne – Frome |
| 07.42 | Bristol Temple Meads – Calne |
| 15.45 SX | Westbury – Calne |
| 17.05 | Westbury – Calne |
| 17.20 | Bristol Temple Meads – Calne |

The last day of passenger services was 18th September 1965, the branch closing from 20th September 1965. Although Calne booking office normally closed at 2 p.m. on a Saturday, on this occasion it was kept open all day to cope with selling hundreds of tickets. The last train, the 10.55 p.m. Saturdays only from Chippenham, normally made the return trip as empty coaching stock but was specially scheduled to depart from Calne at 11.20 p.m. as a passenger-carrying service. Driven by Frank Cannon with Guard Frederick Bond in attendance, more than 140 passengers, including the Mayor and Mayoress of Calne, boarded the 3-car suburban DMU W51134, W59444 and W51147 (now Class 116), which left punctually at 10.55 p.m., exploding detonators. Arriving at Calne, it was greeted by a crowd of over 400. The Last Post was sounded and the train left with flags and streamers hanging from its windows. Between Calne and Black Dog, 102 detonators went off, one for every year the line was in operation. At Black Dog a plaque was mounted on the front of the train. Approaching Chippenham it stopped at the outer home and, after re-starting, the communication cord was pulled and it arrived at Chippenham at 11.46 p.m.

There had been considerable local opposition to closure, but the official explanation was that the whole of the track was life-expired and a culvert near Stanley Bridge Halt was fractured.

Buses proved more expensive. The cheap day return rail fare Calne to Chippenham cost 2s, but a return ticket to Chippenham bus station was 2s 10d and 3s to the railway station. The withdrawal of passenger trains was followed by the withdrawal the following day of Calne's only Sunday morning bus out of the town, the only means of public transport for people visiting hospitals in Bath on Sundays.

Soon after the last train ran, thieves stole miles of telegraph wire. Track lifting started just after Easter 1967 and was completed in June, a short length being left at Chippenham for use as a siding. The bridge over the A4 at Black Dog was removed on 21st April 1968 and Black Bridge over the Avon in 1971.

A 3-car Derby suburban DMU at Calne on 9th September 1965, after the removal of the signals.
*P. Strong*

The Derby suburban 3-car DMU was the last train on the branch, leaving Calne at 11.20 p.m. The notice reads: 'In Memoriam, born 29 October 1863, after giving 101 years of loyal service was killed off 18th September 1965. RIP'.
*P. Pike*